THE TEMP WORKER'S HANDBOOK

William Lewis & Nancy Schuman

THE TEMP WORKER'S HANDBOOK

How to Make Temporary Employment Work for You

amacom

American Management Association

*This book is available at a special
discount when ordered in bulk quantities.
For information, contact Special Sales Department,
AMACOM, a division of American Management Association,
135 West 50th Street, New York, NY 10020.*

LIBRARY OF CONGRESS
Library of Congress Cataloging-in-Publication Data

Lewis, William, 1946–
     *The temp worker's handbook : how to make temporary
employment work for you / William Lewis & Nancy Schuman.*
          p. cm.
     Includes index.
     ISBN 0-8144-7681-3
   *1. Temporary employment—United States—Handbooks,
manuals, etc.*
I. Schuman, Nancy. II. Title.
HD5854.2.U6L48 1988
650.1'4—dc 19   *88–22088*
                                                   CIP

Printing number

10 9 8 7 6 5 4 3 2 1

To Ellen, Carolyn, Ali, and Peggy,
for proving that friendship isn't temporary

ACKNOWLEDGMENTS

The authors would like to thank the following people for their valuable and generous contributions to this book:

- The National Association of Temporary Services and their members, for answering our questions and providing excellent insight into the world of temporary employment.
- Samuel R. Sacco, executive vice-president of the National Association of Temporary Services.
- The National Association of Personnel Consultants, especially Robert M. Allison, chairman, temporary help section.
- Adia Personnel Services, especially Harry Cornelius, vice-president, sales and marketing.
- The gracious and helpful team at Western Temporary Services, Inc.
- Dorothy Walker, reference librarian at Northport Public Library for helping us locate important reference material.
- Terry Fletcher of Temp Connection in New York City for referring us to numerous temps.
- Paul Minx for his bizarre stories about temping.
- Temps everywhere who offered their advice, stories, and experiences.
- All those temporary employment services across the country, and in all fields, who let us pick their brains in order to make this book as informative as possible.
- The Temp Division at Career Blazers' headquarters in New York City, Barbara Cohen, Mary Ellen Graziano, Elisa Morris, Ellyn Weston, and Liz Lam.
- Nancy Brandwein, our editor at AMACOM, for her patience and her commitment to making this book a reality.
- And special praise and gratitude to Ada Alpert, our research assistant, who spent long hours interviewing temps, service personnel, and industry experts to make sure we had the real facts.

Contents

INTRODUCTION /1

1 TEMPING: WHO, WHAT, AND WHY / 5
WHAT IS TEMPING? / 5
WHO IS TEMPING? / 6
    Working Parents / 6
    Students and Recent College Graduates / 7
    Reentry Women / 8
    Artists, Actors, Writers, Musicians / 8
    Retirees / 9
    Job Seekers / 9
    Career Temps / 10
    Professional Temps / 10
    Stereotypical Temps / 11
WHAT MAKES TEMPORARY HELP ATTRACTIVE
   TO BUSINESS? / 11
    Reasons for Using Temporary Help / 12
WHAT MAKES TEMPING ATTRACTIVE TO AN INDIVIDUAL? / 13
    Reasons-to-Temp Checklist / 13
HOW THE TEMP INDUSTRY WORKS / 14
WHAT MAKES A GOOD TEMP? / 15
THE POSITIVE ASPECTS OF TEMPING / 16

IS TEMPING ALWAYS SO TEMPTING? / 17
WEIGHING THE FACTS / 18

2 THE TEMPORARY EMPLOYMENT MARKETPLACE / 19
OFFICE TEMPS / 19
    What Office Skills Are Most in Demand? / 21
    Our Office Salary Survey / 23
    Getting Training Through Your Service / 24
MARKETING TEMPS / 26
INDUSTRIAL TEMPS / 27
MEDICAL TEMPS / 28
    Temporary Nurses / 29
    Home Health Care / 29
TECHNICAL TEMPS / 30
PROFESSIONAL TEMPS / 32

3 PROFESSIONALS—A NEW BREED OF TEMP / 33
DOCTORS: LOCUM TENENS / 34
LAWYERS / 35
INDIAN CHIEFS / 37
FINDING A SERVICE / 39
THE PROS AND CONS / 40

4 YOU AND YOUR SERVICE / 41
CHOOSING A SERVICE / 41
    What They'll Ask You / 47
    What to Ask Them / 48
BUILDING A RELATIONSHIP WITH YOUR SERVICE / 48
    A Word About Attitude / 50
    Some Tips From Assignment Managers / 50
    Accepting an Assignment / 51
    Asking for and Receiving Favors / 51
AT A CLIENT / 53
SENSITIVE ISSUES / 55
    You Hate Your Assignment / 55
    The Temp Working Next to You Earns More per Hour / 57
    A Permanent Employee Wants to Know How Much You Earn / 57
    A Client Wants to Hire You Without Telling Your Service / 58
    Negotiating a Higher Rate / 58
SAMPLE FORMS AND HANDOUTS / 59
WHAT ABOUT BENEFITS? / 60
YOUR RIGHTS AS A TEMP / 65
THE NATIONAL ASSOCIATION OF TEMPORARY SERVICES / 66

5   MY LIFE AS A TEMP / 67
DIARY OF A TEMP, BY PAUL MINX / 67
   To Temp or Not to Temp / 67
   Temp Mama / 68
   Beware the Practical Joker / 69
TEMP PROFILES / 69
   Ghenia Websterss, Brooklyn Heights, New York / 69
   Leslie Fallon, Huntington Beach, California / 70
   James Kennedy, Dallas, Texas / 71
   Anna Marie DeLeyer, St. James, New York / 72
   Susan Press, New York, New York / 73
   Ron Denecour, Mission Viejo, California / 73
   Judie Collard, Greenfield, Wisconsin / 74
   Debbie Schlender-Way, Sunnyvale, California / 75
   Deborah Trotter, San Francisco, California / 75
   Albert Rego, Mission Viejo, California / 76
   Casey Bosco, New York, New York / 77
   April Dillon, East Elmhurst, New York / 77
   Jerry McLoughlin, Bergenfield, New Jersey / 78
   Lorraine Beaulieu, New York, New York / 79
   Tina Clarke, Seattle, Washington / 79
   Jerry Pitts, Phoenix, Arizona / 80
THE BEST AND WORST TEMP ASSIGNMENTS / 80
   The Best / 80
   The Worst / 81

6   THE TEN BIGGEST PROBLEMS OF TEMPING / 82
HOW TO DEAL WITH THE TEMP'S WORST PROBLEMS / 82
   Problem 1: The "Just-a-Temp" Attitude / 82
   Problem 2: The Lack of Benefits / 83
   Problem 3: Social Isolation / 84
   Problem 4: Work Isn't Always Available When You Want It / 85
   Problem 5: Getting Dumped On / 85
   Problem 6: Fighting Boredom / 86
   Problem 7: Adaptability Anxiety / 86
   Problem 8: Acceptance of Your Limited Power / 86
   Problem 9: No Career Path / 87
   Problem 10: Temp Work May Not Be Treated as Credible Work
               Experience / 87

7   ALTERNATIVES TO TEMPING / 89
INTERNAL POOLS OR FLOATERS / 89
PART-TIME EMPLOYMENT / 90

FLEXIBLE WORK SCHEDULES / 92
    Flexitime / 92
    Job Sharing / 92
EMPLOYEE LEASING / 93
PAYROLLING / 94
INDEPENDENT CONTRACTORS / 94

A FINAL WORD / 97

GLOSSARY / 99

DICTIONARY OF TEMPORARY HELP / 105

DIRECTORY OF TEMPORARY SERVICES, BY STATE AND CITY /
  119

**DIRECTORY OF EMPLOYMENT AGENCIES WITH TEMPORARY
SERVICES, BY STATE AND CITY** / 145

INDEX / 153

INTRODUCTION

Today, if you ask someone what he or she does for a living, the unexpected answer might be, "I'm a temp."

Once the exclusive domain of actors and actresses, job hunters, and individuals with unstable employment habits, the field of temporary employment has blossomed into a credible work experience and a conscious career choice for everyone from college graduates to skilled professionals. The "temporary revolution" began in the mid-1980s and mushroomed as more and more businesses and industries changed their perception of temps from crisis fill-ins to personnel to be used as a modern-day management tool. The status of temps continues to be elevated, and few fields (if any) remain as unexplored territory for temporary employees.

If you have always associated this industry with bored housewives, starving actors, or secretaries who pinch-hit while the regular employee is on vacation, you need to be reeducated. Of course, we haven't left yesterday completely behind us; but today you will find temps who are highly skilled, many with college diplomas and advanced degrees. The customer service person at the bank, the nurse who is stepping in to treat you, or the lawyer who has just presented your case is as likely to be a temporary employee as anyone else.

Anna Marie DeLeyer, a personal care nurse's aide, temps because she likes the freedom of her shortened workday, as well as the satisfaction of caring for elderly shut-ins who would otherwise be lost without her help. At age 25, this "career temp" has been in the field for four years.

Herb Moore, an artist and illustrator, temps through a creative service which allows him greater control over his projects, so he can broaden his experiences and creative clout. Says Moore, "It's exciting and stimulating."

Leslie Fallon, a registered pharmacist, temps because she likes the challenge of varied work environments and the opportunity to broaden her professional experiences. She also enjoys the exposure to new patient problems and the chance to expand her range of colleagues.

Ghenia Websterss temps as a personal-computer operator and executive assistant because she wants a respite from a single employer. The experience has allowed her to increase her computer skills and explore the corporate marketplace before committing again to a permanent job. Websterss says it's a wonderful experience for job hunters, because she gets offers for full-time employment wherever she is temping.

Sixty-five-year-old Jerry McLoughlin, a retired CPA, temps as an accountant and says that one of the advantages of temping is that he has profit-sharing benefits at his temporary service. "It's built up a nest egg for me."

These temps are all members of one of the fastest-growing segments of the American workforce. Between 1982 and 1984, the temporary help field increased the number of its employees by 70 percent, making it the fastest-growing industry of those with employment greater than 50,000 members. In 1986, the field employed 786,000 people on a *daily* basis according to the U.S. Bureau of Labor Statistics, and the Bureau predicts that by 1995, the ranks will swell to over one million temps sent out each day.

Why such incredible growth? Possibly the six biggest contributing factors are

- Changing economics
- Shortage of skilled labor
- Increased technology, especially the computerization of the office
- New management trends: adoption of a lean-and-mean philosophy; an attempt to be as recession-proof as possible
- Shift from a product-based economy to a service-based economy
- An effort to reduce hiring costs

All of this is good news to anyone contemplating a stint or a career as a temp. But how do you do it? Is there a right or a wrong way to temp? What are the real advantages and disadvantages of temping; and more importantly, how can you be sure to maximize the field's pluses while minimizing, or at least being aware of, the negatives? That's what this book is about.

As professionals in the temporary employment industry, we have put together information we feel will help you get the most out of temping. While the field has grown dramatically, there is relatively little written about it in book form. It was our belief that potential and existing temps needed a handbook that treated temporary employment as a field in itself and that outlined basic how-to's, the way any career guidance book would for a specific industry. Our project took us to temporary services throughout the United States, where we spoke with industry personnel, temporary employees, and the organizations that use temps on a regular basis. What we learned is all here for us to share with you. In Chapter 1 we examine who today's temps are, what the field is all about, the advantages and disadvantages of temping, and we offer several checklists for you to determine if temping is right for you.

Chapter 2 focuses on the contemporary marketplace for temps and the various skill areas and industries. We discuss the largest segment of the temporary workforce—clerical temps—and how the automated office has influenced employers' needs and related skill levels for temps in this category. We also talk about training for the automated office and how to obtain marketable skills. A national salary survey is included for positions within an office environment.

Chapter 3 offers a new dimension in the temporary employment industry: the use of professional temps such as doctors, lawyers, engineers, chemists, architects, and technical employees. We had not planned this chapter when we began writing, but our research and interviews proved that this was a growing and significant area, and needed to be addressed.

Chapter 4 tells you how to work best with a temp service. How can you be assured of the best assignments? We also include a sampling of forms you are likely to encounter as a temp, such as a time sheet and employment application. We discuss how to ask a temp service for a raise and how to turn down assignments without jeopardizing your employment opportunities with your service. We also include the types of fringe benefits you can expect as a temp, as well as your rights as a temporary employee.

Chapter 5 is filled with feedback from people who are currently temping. You'll learn what hints they can offer and how temping fits into their life-styles.

We've called Chapter 6 "The Ten Biggest Problems of Temping," and we tell you how to deal with them.

Chapter 7 discusses alternatives to temping, such as temping without a service, job sharing, and working as an independent contractor.

You will also find a glossary of terms prepared by The National Association of Temporary Services, reprinted with its permission. This should prove helpful in providing a clear definition of words you may encounter in your experience as a temp. Adia Personnel Services has kindly allowed us to include its *Dictionary of Temporary Help,* which provides job descriptions for various positions in the temporary help industry.

Two very valuable directories conclude the book. One has been prepared by The National Association of Temporary Services; it lists its members by city and state. The other was designed by The National Association of Personnel Consultants, and includes a roster of its members who offer temporary help services, as well as an employment agency division for obtaining permanent employment.

As a temp, you wield a considerable amount of power. The temporary help service you are working for needs you to make it look good to its client companies. You also have maximum control of your workday. It is up to you to choose when you want to work and where. What you do with all your power and control is up to you. Many believe that being an exceptional temp is an art form. Those who have mastered it say there is no greater satisfaction than feeling like a hero whenever they come in and save the day. Our book can't make you a great temp—only you can do that. However, we can help you perfect your technique with our inside information. Our advice is for you to approach your experience as a temp with your eyes open and a clear understanding of what to expect and what you want to get out of it. For many, temporary employment offers permanent career satisfaction. We wish you every success as a temporary employee.

Chapter 1

TEMPING: WHO, WHAT, AND WHY

Thinking about temporary employment? Good for you. Those people who continue to casually dismiss temping as a bohemian life-style or as a career choice for the inept, semiskilled, or unstable don't know what you know—that temping has become a popular choice for individuals in all fields and of all ages, and that employers have new attitudes toward the importance of temporary help and its use in business.

The temporary help field is quite unlike any other in the scope of its complexity. It is actually an industry consisting of many industries. Temporary help can be classified in any one of four categories: office, industrial, medical, and technical/professional. Under these four banner heads are numerous job titles and occupations. The temporary help industry is the only one where construction workers, chemists, X-ray technicians, and switchboard operators can all fall under the management of a single employer—a temporary help service.

WHAT IS TEMPING?

In simplest terms, temping is working for a temporary help firm that pays you an hourly wage and all the costs associated with employment: insurance, FICA, disability, worker's compensation, fringe benefits, and so on. The temporary service sends you out on short- or long-term assignments at one of their client organizations, and the client is billed an hourly charge for your services. A temporary employee is *never* the employee of the organization, individual, or business where he or she is fulfilling an assignment. A temporary employee is *always* the employee of the temporary help firm which sends the temp out.

Let's take a look at the breakdown of personnel within the four categories of temporary help. Not surprisingly, the leader is office personnel, where you'll find 63 percent of the total annual temporary payroll. Following office is industrial/labor, with a 15.8 percent share of the population; health care, with 10.8 percent; and technical/professional, not far behind with 10.4 percent. When you consider that 10.4 percent represents almost 80,000 professional/technical temps employed in any given day, even that number becomes significant.

A temporary help service is unique in structure because it is both a private-sector business and a labor intermediary. As a private-sector business, it has its own market and sells its product to a variety of customers. As a labor intermediary, a temporary help service can have considerable influence on the supply and demand of the customers it serves.

Organizations utilize temporary help to meet emergency staffing needs and to gain flexibility in staffing without incurring the costs associated with the hiring and maintenance of permanent staff. A business could function without the services of a temporary help firm, but most find it preferable to contract out rather than take on the task themselves. Such contracting can range from a request for a one-day typist to an extensive contract for an entire shift of food and beverage workers; this type of contract may be put out for competitive bidding to a number of temporary help firms.

The good news is that because temporary help has become such a constant in business, the list of job categories filled by temps has broadened extensively. The business community is quickly learning that there are not very many categories of workers that the temporary help industry cannot provide. You'll find on the payroll of a temporary help firm everyone from an assembly-line worker to a lawyer. The nationwide shortage of qualified personnel has opened up temping to just about everyone.

WHO IS TEMPING?

Maybe the more appropriate question is, Who *isn't* temping? The overwhelming growth in the temp industry has radically changed the image and expectations of those individuals who are labeled *temps*.

Here's just a sampling of people who are finding that temporary work has definite advantages.

Working Parents

More often than not, these are working mothers (two thirds of the temporary population are women) who find that the flexibility of temporary work suits their hectic schedules and allows them to meet family responsibilities. In between car pools, scouting, Little League, and home life, temporary work is an excellent way to enjoy a career and care for children and a spouse. Some parents work two or three days a week, some more, some less, again, when you temp, the choice is yours. Even more convenient is the ability to take off for children's vacations, whether during the school year or summer. Some working mothers tell us that knowing they can be home if a child is ill and not feel guilty about missing a day of work is a real sanity-saver.

Some women report that by working as temps, they feel that they can "have it all" without burning out. Elaine Cartwright reserves every Thursday and Friday as her work days to temp. A former public relations executive, Cartwright, who is 36 years old, left her $28,000-a-year position six years ago to have a family.

I missed the stimulation of work, but I didn't want to sacrifice the time with my sons to resume a full-time career . . . I have friends who are still working the long and crazy hours I used to work before motherhood. . . . I don't want to be superwoman, but I do like having both a job and a home life. . . . I think, like most women in the eighties, I felt tremendous external and internal pressure to have both an interesting career and a loving family. I found that temping is the easiest way to make this a reality and keep everyone happy.

Students and Recent College Graduates

Temping was not traditionally a safe route for recent graduates, yet the eighties has made this path not only a safe one but almost a trend. Today, graduates are opting for temp work as an answer to several employment dilemmas. It is an opportunity to explore industries and specific companies, and get an all-important foot in the door at their ideal employer. Very often, competition is high at choice organizations for entry-level positions; but an individual who comes in as a temp not only gets to test the waters for himself or herself but has an opportunity to show a firm what he or she can do. Temporary positions can and do lead to permanent employment, but the choice is yours. Students also like temping in order to build some credible business experience apart from typical college-held jobs, such as lifeguarding, and cashier. Says one graduate,

I built an impressive roster of work references through temping. When I went on the interview for the job I really wanted and could say my references were from two big-name ad agencies (both from temp assignments), I knew I had the job.

Valerie Jacobsen temped while getting her MBA at Indiana University. Jacobsen used her temping experience almost as if it were a corporate internship.

The people I worked with saw beyond my typing skills. When they asked me why I was temping, and wasn't I overqualified for the work I was doing, I didn't hesitate to tell them my background. I also told them I was there to see the inner workings of a successful company, and this type of firsthand experience can't be taught in business school.

Jacobsen's assigned employer kept her on for an eight-week, July through August, assignment. "Originally, it was just for three days; but we liked each other. I got to do some interesting things like preparing budgets and checking over financial reports."

Reentry Women

Many women are returning to the workforce, either by choice or from necessity. The easiest and fastest way to building confidence and skills is through temping. A woman who has been out of the labor force for as little as three years has a great deal of technology to catch up with. Returnees who haven't worked for many years are often nervous and anxious about reentering the workplace. Temping is a way to ease the trauma of the career experience: Facing a job is a little less terrifying if it is only one or two days a week, near home, and sounds like something she wants to do. As a temp, a returnee can brush up on old skills (rusty, but not completely forgotten) and, more importantly, learn the fine points of the automated office. One returnee reported to us that she learned word processing while on an assignment.

I sort of taught myself at someone else's expense. When I first started working, using a complicated copier was scary enough; but electronic mail was a complete unknown! I temped and learned a little at a time. I never would have made it if I jumped right into a full-time position. Temping gave me confidence and skills.

Artists, Actors, Writers, Musicians

Anyone in the arts is usually familiar with the benefits of temporary work. Why? Well, it is a sure way to pay the rent when you are making the rounds between auditions. Individuals whose first love happens to be writing, acting, or singing discovered temping long ago. And organizations are usually only too happy to have them come aboard as temps. Those who are creatively gifted are often verbal, look good, and have developed highly efficient skills. You'll find them in traditional office positions, but they are also the ones willing to try something outrageous. One New York City actor/temp dressed as Pinocchio for a famous toy store's promotion, and on another occasions he was a "body" in a casket display for a morticians convention.

We also learned of a group of five actors (three men and two women) who shared a large Manhattan brownstone. The temp service they worked for referred to them as *The House*. All five individuals had excellent office skills; and when a temp was needed for an assignment, the service called The House and left a message on their machine. One of the five was always available; and if several were available, they would draw straws.

Retirees

This is a new group to discover the temporary labor market, and they are being well received by temporary help firms and their clients alike. Their reasons for working are fairly obvious: to supplement a fixed income, to enjoy some mental stimulation, and to have the opportunity to feel as though they can continue to make a contribution. Companies say they are all for senior citizens as temps because they are reliable and possess an old-fashioned work ethic.

In 1987 Kelly Services, Inc., one of the nation's largest temporary services, instituted a program aimed directly at recruiting individuals aged 55 and older. Kelly calls its program Encore!℠ and says that of Kelly's 525,000 temporary employees, approximately 35,000 are over age 55. Kelly Services has also been included in an American Association of Retired Persons (AARP) computerized directory that provides examples of employment programs for older workers.

Many of the seniors registered with temporary help services are people who were forced into retirement because they had reached their firm's mandatory retirement age. Some of these same people never leave their posts, though, because their firm retains them, not on the company payroll, but on that of a temporary help service through a feature commonly known as *payrolling*.

One happy senior we spoke with told us that retirement for him meant an opportunity to travel, and that not only did occasional temporary jobs enable him to have an extra cash reserve for his trips but that he often temped while travelling. His paychecks supplemented his pension and didn't hamper his receiving Social Security benefits. At the time of this writing, the law permits a senior (under 65) to earn up to $6,120 annually without jeopardizing his or her Social Security pension. Those 65 and older may earn $8,400 and still receive all of their benefits. A senior can earn more than these figures; however, there is a deduction of $1 in the pension for every $2 earned. Most older employees simply stop temping when they reach their earning's limit. Individuals who are 70 plus will get their full Social Security benefit each month no matter how much they earn.

Job Seekers

One person out of five who temps is looking for a permanent job. People who temp in order to secure a permanent position quickly become familiar with what is commonly known as the hidden job market. As a temporary employee, you will be exposed to the estimated 60 percent of job openings that go unadvertised. Many organizations hope to fill internal positions by promoting from within. Your inside edge puts you close to the decision-makers with hiring authority. Job seekers recognize that temping allows them to explore such things as work environments, specific firms, and whether or not they like the responsibilities associated with a particular position; and it allows them to test themselves with new challenges. If you have just moved to a new city, temporary employment may be the ideal way to learn the ins and outs of your new marketplace. Or, perhaps you want to switch fields. The transition may be much smoother if you temp first to ensure that you really like the field you want to get involved in and to see if your real-world experiences match up with your expectations.

Because so many people do become permanent employees as a result of the temporary assignments, temp services report that one of their biggest problems is attrition. "We lose a lot of good people to our clients," says one representative at a temporary help service. "A company doesn't necessarily place an order with the hope of finding someone permanent; sometimes it just happens. . . . Often, the chemistry is right."

Career Temps

These are workers who have turned temporary employment into a full-time career.

You get hooked on the freedom of this life-style. It's very addictive. If it's a beautiful day, I go to the beach instead of to the office, and no one has a problem with it. Usually my temp service is thrilled to hear from me after a two-day work reprieve. I also like going in and doing a great job, especially if the company isn't expecting a temp with brains. It's great to prove them wrong. A lot of the firms I've temped at request me back by name.

Career temporaries are occasionally referred to as *professional* temps. This can be very confusing, since temporaries are filling more and more technical (professional) types of openings. For the purpose of clarity, we will always refer to full-time temporary workers as *career temps*.

When people make a career out of temping, it does not mean that they can't find permanent work or that they are unstable, irresponsible employees. Most get job offers frequently; they simply choose not to say yes. For career temps, temping is their livelihood. They report with satisfaction that the advantages of temporary employment far outweigh the negatives.

Professional Temps

Contemporary corporate culture stresses fast-track careerism. Old-fashioned company loyalty has given way to workers who want a successful career, yet want to pursue individual freedoms. This way of thinking has let a whole group of professionals, such as attorneys, doctors, chemists, engineers, computer specialists, accountants, and senior-level executives (in a variety of fields), discover that temping can be an acceptable, as well as an emotionally satisfying and financially rewarding, career route. Ground-breakers in these fields have helped to give credibility to an employment pattern previously unthinkable for such professions. It is the era of the entrepreneur; and although professional temps do work through a service, many function as though they were independent businesspeople. "I run my own show," says one such temp. "I put the pressure on myself to work; there's no one boss looking over my shoulder to check my progress."

Stereotypical Temps

We would be denying a basic reality if we didn't admit that there are still temps who are everything the public perceives them to be. Yes, they are irresponsible, they can't hold down permanent jobs; in short, they're a bit flaky. However, you may encounter this personality no matter where you work, be it a permanent job or a temporary assignment. Such people naturally gravitate toward temping because it is structured around their idiosyncrasies. The good news is that the temporary help field is now being actively sought out by people who traditionally would have chosen permanent positions, thus elevating the caliber of the temporary employee. Unfortunately, employers have lived with the stereotypical temp for some time, and many expect the worst when a temp walks through the door. We suggest that you make the most out of this situation. Your work habits and abilities will make you an immediate star.

WHAT MAKES TEMPORARY HELP ATTRACTIVE TO BUSINESS?

Industry experts put the number of temporary help firms at over 7,600 in the United States alone. This includes everything from the mom-and-pop shop to the well-known industry giants and their branches or franchise offices. Much of the temporary help industry's expanded popularity and use in staff management is in response to the layoffs and staff cutbacks of the 1981–1982 economic recession. Organizations began implementing lean-and-mean management styles by advocating the use of temporary staff rather than risk hiring permanent personnel. Temps represent no extra expenditures. A slowdown no longer represents a layoff—it simply means a temporary work assignment has ended. More and more companies budget temporary employees to the purchasing department as a labor expense rather than to a specific department's personnel budget. The company benefits from purchasing specific labor costs rather than incurring severance costs when a peak work period is over. Businesses cannot afford to maintain large labor pools with employees of every skill category and then use these workers' skills sporadically. Today, it is typical to find a core of key permanent employees surrounded by a staff of temporary employees who fill in on an as-needed basis. For most businesses, the supplier of these temporary employees is a temporary help service with its army of temps ready to step in for a half day or a full year or more. During our research, we learned of one temp who has been temping at the same assignment for seven years.

Another reason for the enormous growth in the temporary help field is the changing face of the office that results from new technology. The automated office has created a real demand for skilled equipment specialists and operators. Temporary help services as well as individual employers are currently competing heavily for this category of worker.

Traditional uses for temporary help continue to remain a constant in business. Companies still call on a temporary service for quick-fix replacements for ill or vacationing employees, and to handle seasonal needs or one-time projects. According to the Administrative Management Society, nine out of ten businesses now use temporary help at least once a year.

The tremendous growth of the temp industry is also due in part to changing labor factors. Businesses are having difficulty finding the personnel they need because of several shifting factors. First, the women's movement has enabled women who previously might have gone into supporting roles to move into the management sector. Furthermore, the aging of the workforce causes a lack of sufficient lower-level young workers to meet the demand. We have also seen the decline of the traditional secretarial school, which has put increased pressure on businesses to cross-train existing personnel on a variety of office equipment and requires administrators to absorb some of the clerical overload. Finally, increased labor-force mobility means that fewer people are staying at the same jobs for long periods of time; job-hopping has become more acceptable; and with workers spending less time in a position, companies are forced constantly to hire and retrain staff.

Reasons for Using Temporary Help

Here are some of the reasons why client companies use temporary help. (They are not listed in order of frequency or importance.)

- Vacation replacement
- Illness or temporary absence of permanent staff
- Unexpected quits or terminations of permanent staff
- Peak work loads
- Seasonal demand
- Supplement to permanent staff
- Specialized work

- One-time project
- Possible permanency
- To reduce personnel overhead
- Fluctuating business cycles
- Disasters, such as bankruptcy, flood, or fire
- Merger
- Company relocation
- Purchase of new equipment

WHAT MAKES TEMPING ATTRACTIVE TO AN INDIVIDUAL?

Although we have attempted to list several categories of individuals who find temp work an attractive option, the field is in no way confined to these groups. Others who enjoy the freedom and the flexibility this type of career provides include teachers during semester breaks, students, flight attendants, people who earn gift money during the September-through-Christmas period, and spouses of military personnel. Here are nineteen good reasons to temp; see if one or more appeal to you.

Reasons-to-Temp Checklist

☐ I like the adventure of working at different companies and in different industries.

☐ I can earn more money per hour as a temp.

☐ I can meet new people, friends and business contacts.

☐ I'm new to the area; temping is an opportunity to become familiar with the city and its businesses.

☐ I don't want the commitment of a full-time job.

☐ I want to work only a few days a week.

☐ I'd like to earn money while on vacation or while traveling.

☐ I'm between jobs and want to use temping as a means to explore fields, companies, and new experiences.

☐ I'm in a city for a limited stay and need to earn an income.

☐ I want to return to work, and temping is a good way to get my feet wet and see how the workplace has changed.

☐ I'm retired, but I'd like to work when I feel the need.

☐ I'm a performer/artist/writer, and I need flexible hours and an income to pursue my first love.

☐ I'm a student, and temp work can be arranged around my class schedule so that I can earn some money easily while going to school.

☐ I think I'd like to work at this company, but I'm not sure. If I temp, I can have a trial period before committing to permanent employment.

☐   I want to be in control of my career; I don't like feeling I can be manip-
      ulated by an employer.

☐   I want a sense of freedom, to play hooky or do what I want on the days I
      want to do it.

☐   I can earn the income I want without the pressures and politics of a
      traditional career.

☐   I have children and I want to be home with them when they are not in
      school.

☐   I want a permanent position, and temporary jobs can make me visible to
      an employer.

   Do any of these sound good to you? If so, you may be a prime candidate for
temporary employment.

HOW THE TEMP INDUSTRY WORKS

In order to be a temporary employee, you should have a good understanding
of the industry basics. Temporary help firms recruit and screen applicants for
temporary jobs. These jobs are listed with the service and are generally from
businesses in the surrounding area. Typically, the orders for these workers are
placed one or two days in advance; but there are many instances in which
orders are for the same day because a customer needs a temp immediately.
Such quick turnaround requires a large and current pool of qualified temps, so
that the customer may be served quickly and efficiently. The usual way a temporary help service recruits temps is by advertisement, referral incentives, and
word of mouth. Potential temps are screened, tested in certain skill areas,
requested to provide names of references, and interviewed by a representative
from the temporary service. Often, the service will categorize temps by skill
levels and qualifications so that when an order comes in, it is easy to find an
appropriate temp. The temporary service hires, fires, issues paychecks, with-
holds necessary taxes, makes employer contributions to Social Security and
Unemployment, and may offer fringe benefits to their temps at their own dis-
cretion.

   The temporary service is paid by the client (the business or individual re-
quiring the temp) on an hourly basis. In turn, the temporary help service pays
their employee (the temp) also at an hourly rate. Generally, the service charges
the client anywhere from a 35 percent to a 60 percent markup for the services
of the temporary employee. While this may appear high, businesses usually
justify the price by noting what they save on employee recruitment costs, insurance, fringe benefits, overtime, severance, and any possible subsequent
unemployment insurance. You should also remember that the temp service is

paying these same costs out of their markup, as well as additional costs such as insurance for bonding temps and errors and omissions insurance, which protects the temporary service in case the temp does something tremendously harmful to a client while on an assignment.

Most firms are sold on the concept of using temporary employees. In fact, a survey of 800 companies in twelve major cities reported that they spend an average of $64,000 a year on temporary labor with 10 percent of the companies spending an average of $225,000 a year on temps.

WHAT MAKES A GOOD TEMP?

In writing this book, we spoke with representatives from over sixty temporary services throughout the United States. The overwhelming response to this question was **flexibility.** Terry Hueneke, senior vice-president and group executive at Manpower Inc., one of the world's largest temporary services, summed it up best:

> *A great temp possesses a motivated, positive work attitude. He or she is flexible, able to adapt quickly to new situations . . . someone who is inquisitive and is not intimidated when faced with the unknown. A great temp operates under a positive work ethic . . . hard work, timeliness, punctuality, and understands his or her commitment to the temp service and the corporate client.*

Review some of the other characteristics from our survey to see how you compare with what those in the industry cited as desirable traits.

- ☐ Adaptable, flexible to new people and situations.
- ☐ Self-disciplined, able to motivate self without any external pressure.
- ☐ Unflustered and unbothered by the nonroutine.
- ☐ A good communicator; will keep in touch with the temp service and be unafraid to ask questions at an assignment.
- ☐ Likes autonomy in work.
- ☐ Agreeable to the nonideal—not every assignment will be what you want.
- ☐ Possesses excellent interpersonal skills.
- ☐ A desire to continually learn and improve skills.
- ☐ Possesses a good sense of humor.
- ☐ Reliable, punctual, and responsible.

Before you go into a temporary help service to register for employment, sit down and think about what you want to get out of the experience. Ask yourself why you want to temp, how long you think you will temp, and what kind of work are you looking for. Come to terms with these things yourself, and then be able to verbalize the answers out loud. Your temp service should know what you want and what you expect if you would like to have a mutually beneficial relationship with them.

THE POSITIVE ASPECTS OF TEMPING

Boardroom Reports, in New York City, recently stated that 57 percent of the temps they polled in a formal survey found their life-style more challenging than one that would be provided by traditional employment. Fifty percent reported that temporary work meets all of their financial obligations.

You don't have to be a gypsy to enjoy temporary employment; and if you enjoy it, don't feel guilty about it. Temping is legitimate work and is losing many of the old stigmas it once had. Temps who temp for the freedom and flexibility wouldn't change their life for permanent employment. Temps who temp to supplement their household income say it provides vacation money and otherwise unobtainable luxuries. If you plan to temp because you are seeking a permanent job, temp at a service which has an employment agency affiliate. Often, you can register for both permanent and temporary employment at the same time, and you will be more likely to be sent on assignments that have a good chance of converting to permanent status. Your agency counselor will work with the temp service representative to set up interviews and assignments around your work schedule. If you are contemplating a permanent job with a specific industry or employer, do some sleuthing while you are on your temp assignment.

- [ ] Is the office atmosphere frantic or laid-back?
- [ ] Who are the people in power? What are they like?
- [ ] Does the permanent staff seem happy? How is morale?
- [ ] Which departments are currently hiring?
- [ ] What is the pay scale like? How about benefits?

We firmly believe that proximity is the mother of opportunity. Once you are on the inside of a company you may at least be perceived as "one of them." You'll find that executives will speak to you more freely, and if they like your work habits, it's easy to ask for some career guidance. One paralegal we spoke with developed a mentor at a long-term assignment. He is now attending law school while still working as a permanent temporary at the same law firm. Other job hunters tell us they are less pressed during their job search when they are temping and have a source of income. Temping also enables them to have employment continuity—they are still part of the work force and have a reason to get up and get dressed. It gives an individual a sense of momentum. Here are some other responses from satisfied temps.

> *My husband was on disability and we needed more money, so I temped and stopped when he was well.*
>
> *I escaped a lousy job situation through temping till I could find a new permanent job.*
>
> *Work isn't my life; temping lets me do those things that are really important to me.*
>
> *The pay is good.*
>
> *I temp by night and work full time by day.*
>
> *I temp five months a year: September through November for my Christmas money and February through March for our summer vacation.*

IS TEMPING ALWAYS SO TEMPTING?

No.

Most of the temps we interviewed told us temping is a mix of positive and negative experiences. And most had come to terms with this trade-off.

Susan Grady told us, "There are days when I feel like I put my brain in a basement." Grady spoke of supervisors at a client's office who were unprepared and unable to supervise a temp, managers who didn't know what they wanted or where anything was. Other temps told us that they occasionally felt isolated and left out of company events. We learned of one temp who was hurt because she was not invited to the office Christmas party even though she had been on the assignment at the firm for over seven months. "It wasn't company policy; they said if they did it for one, they would have to do it for all."

Temping does have its disadvantages: social isolation from co-workers; the subjection to the "just a temp" attitude; and many temp services still do not provide health insurance and other fringe benefits to their employees. We discuss these and other problems in greater detail in Chapter 6.

Of course, the temporary help industry is not without its critics. Some sociologists call temps working nomads. They maintain that we are creating a disposable employment force, which is unhealthy for workers as well as organizations. Critics argue that the lack of camaraderie between temps and permanent staff creates an isolated environment. They believe that the continued use of temporary employees causes the corporate culture to suffer on account of a transient staff which feels no loyalty to the organization and operates with no organizational memory. Labor advocates are also concerned that temps will be used increasingly to break strikes. Many temporary services do observe a policy of not crossing picket lines, but a company can legally replace striking employees with temporary employees.

WEIGHING THE FACTS

Temping can give you the best of several worlds. Like any career choice it has its ups and downs, and understanding them will help make your decision to temp easier. Fortunately, you can get in and out of temping without too much trouble. For that reason, we feel it is an option people should consider, especially if they enjoy freedom, independence, and the opportunity to explore new work environments on a regular basis.

Chapter **2**

THE TEMPORARY EMPLOYMENT MARKETPLACE

Temporary jobs are generally categorized in four basic employment groups:

1. Office
2. Industrial
3. Medical
4. Technical/Professional

While a local temporary service may serve more than one of the above groups, it is more likely to concentrate on a single sector. Some of the larger services and national firms address several or all of the four groups, but usually this is accomplished by separate divisions or subsidiaries.

OFFICE TEMPS

Clearly, the largest number of temporary jobs fall into the office category. Clerical help is rarely cyclical or seasonal; it is a constant in business. A sampling of occupational titles in this area follows, in approximate order from lowest- to highest-paying positions. (This does not represent a complete listing).

File Clerk	Administrative Assistant
General Clerk	Secretary with Word Processing or
Mailroom Clerk	PC skills
Records Clerk	Accounts Payable
Legal Clerk	Accounts Receivable
Accounting Clerk	Assistant Bookkeeper
Switchboard Operator	Full Charge Bookkeeper
Receptionist	Entry-level Word Processing
Receptionist with Typing	Operator
Clerk Typist	Word Processing Operator
Typist	Personal Computer (PC) Operator
Transcription Typist	Advanced Operator
Statistical Typist	Systems Administrator/Supervisor
Proofreader	Trainer
Secretary	Data Entry Clerk
Bilingual Secretary	Data Processing Operator
Executive Secretary	Spreadsheet Operator
Legal Secretary	Data-base Management

The forecasted growth and demand for skilled office support personnel is exceedingly high, particularly for information processing temps. A study by Xerox Corporation showed that a word processing or PC station is currently on one out of every five office desks and that by 1989, three out of five is predicted.

Computerization was the real catalyst for the growth of the temporary help industry. The increased technology created a "Catch-22" in the workplace. In the late 1970s and early 1980s, companies purchased equipment which could speed up office operations, but they lacked the "people" power and know-how to make it happen. The staffing dilemma of the typist who was forced to become a word-processor or PC operator happened too quickly for most organizations; and to keep up productivity, they turned to outside help. Temporary services began supplying qualified office automation operators and changed the face of the temporary help industry forever. In an effort to expand the temp industry's labor pool, many firms set up training divisions. Their goal was to train unskilled temps, as well as to upgrade and cross-train temps with existing skills, thus increasing the overall supply of available temps. Many temps became better versed in the use of the machinery and software than the permanent employees. The mid-1980s saw the rise in the use of conversion teams, a team of temps who came into an office to set up the equipment and systems for the permanent staff and then trained them in its use. Temps quickly learned that the fastest way to an increased paycheck was by learning to operate a word-processor or PC. Today, it is not unusual for a temp to be fluent in several of the most popular software packages. The difficulty is that the technology changes so rapidly that state of the art means something new every week.

Of all the office job orders received by temporary services daily, an estimated 80 to 85 percent require some degree of office automation skills. *The New York Times* reports that between 20 and 30 million letters are written, typed/inputted, and mailed each day. We believe that much of this is accomplished with the help of temporary employees.

What Office Skills Are Most in Demand?

Although the use of specific equipment varies around the country, it is the general consensus that any word processing, PC, and typing skills command immediate attention. Terry Hueneke of Manpower Inc. tells us:

There has been a shift in terminology from word processing to text processing. This indicates a shift in the market from the dedicated word processor to the personal computer and midrange or mainframe computer with a PC or terminal as a work station. Skill requests are for more than straight word of text processing: clients also need electronic spreadsheet, data base, and data entry skills, such as calendaring, scheduling, and electronic mail. These requests mirror an evolution of equipment in the marketplace.

We asked temp services nationwide what were their most frequent personal requests for computer software packages. Here is what they said, not in any particular order of popularity. (The following terms are all trademarks.)

MultiMate	Microsoft Word
MultiMate Advantage	Lotus 1-2-3
WordPerfect	dBase III
WordStar	dBase III Plus
WordStar Professional	Symphony
WordStar 2000	Multiplan
IBM DisplayWrite 3	PageMaker
IBM DisplayWrite 4	

If these names hold a lot of mystery for you, you are probably not currently temping in an office environment. If you are unfamiliar with what a personal computer can do, you need to educate yourself about the automated office. We suggest that you visit a computer store, one that sells home and business equipment, and ask for a demonstration (on the pretext of buying). You will be amazed at the capabilities of these desk-top wizards. You may also investigate several trade publications written for computer industry personnel; some of these titles may be available at your local library. While the actual content of these magazines may be too complicated for the novice, you can pick up important buzzwords and examine photographs of the most recent technology.

PC *Magazine*, published biweekly by Ziff-Davis Publishing Co., a division
of Ziff Communications Co., 1 Park Avenue, New York, NY 10016.
PC *World*, published monthly by PCW Communications, Inc., 501 Second
Street, San Francisco, CA 94107.
Office Administration and Automation, published monthly by Geyer-
McAllister Publications, Inc., 51 Madison Avenue, New York, NY
10010.
The Office, published monthly by Office Publications, Inc., 1600 Summer
Street, Stamford, CT 06904.

For your own reference we offer a *very* simplified definition of a personal
computer: It is a small computer system capable of accomplishing a variety of
tasks. It can perform word processing functions, which allow you to create text
on a screen and then manipulate the text to your liking without erasures, mis-
spellings, or fuss. An operator can transpose words, delete pieces of text,
change words, copy whole sections of text, repaginate, and much more, just by
touching the keyboard. A personal computer also allows you the ability to do
spreadsheet functions; that is, the electronic processing of numbers. Rather
than use a traditional pencil and ledger sheet, an operator can key in financial
information and display it on the screen. The computer can do all basic math,
as well as produce graphs and charts. A PC can also be a data-base management
system, which permits the operator to create and manipulate a collection of
information organized by a particular method. There are all kinds of data-base
files, but a telephone book is a tangible example. Lastly, the newest use for a
PC is desktop publishing, which enables an operator to create, illustrate, and
design everything from newsletters to catalogs, and more. All of this is done
with special software packages that remove the need for cutting, pasting, and
traditional production of mechanicals.

Probably the best advice for a new office temp is to take as many entry-level
assignments as possible, maximizing your current skills. Get inside a firm and
look at everything. And try as many different fields as possible. Different
industries make different uses of office automation. High-volume users include insurance, law, and real estate firms; advertising agencies, securities and
health-care companies, and banks. Often, you can learn on the job. You can
also register with a temporary service that provides free training to temps who
work a specific number of hours for them. This will be discussed in more detail
just a bit later in this chapter.

Typing is an old, reliable standby skill. Of course, if you haven't been in an
office for over ten years, you will still experience a wave of shock at how this
old friend has been modernized. There are both electric and electronic typewriters. Most people are familiar with the electric models. Electronic typewriters are the step before the word processor. It is a machine with a shorter

memory than a word processor; thus, it generally can only store information ranging from one line to several pages of text, while word processing systems are capable of storing hundreds of pages at one time. An electronic typewriter can, however, automatically handle tabulations, margins, centering, underlining, and erasures at the touch of a key.

Our Office Salary Survey

How do you know you are getting paid what you are worth? Your newspaper classifieds are one of your best resources. Don't just check ads under "Temporary Help"; review columns such as Accounting, Administrative Assistant, Clerical, Computer, Gal/Guy Friday, Secretary, Typist, and Word Processing. Ads for permanent jobs can help you compute a fair market hourly rate, and of course, you'll want to check out what a variety of temporary services are offering to pay. Our informal survey of temporary services around the country revealed the typical hourly rate ranges shown in the accompanying table.

	Receptionist	Secretary	Sec'y w/Steno	WP/PC Oper.
New York	$5.20–8.50	$7.00–13.00	$ 9.00–14.00	$ 8.50–18.00+
Boston	5.00–8.00	7.00–11.00	10.00–13.00	10.00–15.00
Chicago	5.50–8.00	7.00–10.00	10.00–12.00	8.00–17.00
Denver	5.25–7.50	7.00– 9.00	8.00–10.00	8.00–13.00
Los Angeles	6.00–8.00	8.00– 9.00	9.00–12.00	8.00–14.00+
Houston	5.50–7.00	6.50– 8.00	7.50–11.00	8.00–13.00
Philadelphia	4.25–7.50	5.50– 9.00	6.50–10.00	8.50–16.00
Milwaukee	4.50–5.75	5.00– 6.00	6.00– 8.00	7.00–10.00+
Miami	5.00–6.50	7.00– 9.00	8.00–14.00	8.00–12.00+

It is important that you understand several key points about your pay rate. First, it is typical for a service to start you out at the low end of the rate range when you are a new employee. Since you are an unproven entity, a temp service will want feedback from its clients on your job performance. Second, different assignments pay different rates. You can make $9.50 per hour one week and drop to $9.25 per hour the next week. The temp service pays you based on what they are billing the client. Third, once you master a new skill, don't expect to jump to a much higher pay rate immediately. Client companies may be reluctant to let a newly trained operator test the waters on their premises. Your temp service may market you to their client as an entry-level or junior operator so you can build up several assignments of hands-on experience. Experience and skills are the keys to a bigger paycheck. Finally, if you are sent to a company to do reception work and you find yourself doing reception *and* typing, tell your temporary service. This is the kind of information they need to know to ensure you a proper hourly rate and to charge the company an appropriate figure for the work you are doing. Always tell your service when your responsibilities are upgraded from what you were originally told the assignment would entail. Ultimately, you can expect from $2 to $6 an hour *more* for your new skill.

Getting Training Through Your Service

There are two distinct points of view on whether temp services need to provide office skills training for their employees. Some services feel that by training they are able to expand their labor pool and can fill a wider range of job orders. Other services maintain they are temporary services, not trainers. They feel that if they do provide training, they are investing a considerable amount of money in a temp who may stay in their employ just long enough to get the training. These firms concentrate on attracting temps with existing skills, often by paying higher hourly rates.

Training at temporary services can cover such skills as operation of personal computers, machine transcription, accounting, and telemarketing. If you think you can benefit by way of training, actively seek out a firm that offers such a program to its employees. Joyce Ostrander, president of Temp Careers, Inc., in Buffalo, New York, explains:

> *We provide training on the IBM personal computer. We utilize tutorial programs for MultiMate, Lotus 1-2-3, and Symphony. Our only requirement is that the temp needs to be a good typist and either possesses some computer savvy or, at least, is not be afraid of a computer. We take the cream of the crop from our office files. . . . We look for someone who will be a long-term asset to our company. Generally, these are people who have worked for us for some time, but that's not a prerequisite. . . . Our training is purely discretionary.*

At Star Temps, the oldest local temporary service in the Miami area, Patti Ragan, president, offers, "We provide training for equipment in our office, as well as at other sources. . . . We've gone outside to train because it is impossible to have all the necessary equipment here. . . . We've made a commitment to train so we can send out qualified people." One of Star's programs, a legal secretarial course, is offered through Florida International University. "We pay 50 percent of the tuition, and if a temp works for us one month, they can work off the remaining 50 percent payment for the course," says Ragan.

Some temporary services have written and designed their own personal computer software training. This can range from a few hours to a twenty-hour course. Further, some services provide actual IBM PCs or compatibles, while others offer training on systems that simulate various word processing equipment and software packages. At Kelly Services, Inc., one of the largest and best-known national services, training is provided on computer simulators that electronically score the accuracy of their operators. The computer has three modes of operation: one to demonstrate, one to guide the worker throughout the exercise, and one to test operator competency. Kelly also provides a toll-free hotline for its temps in case they find themselves in a difficult position during an assignment.

Manpower Inc. has invested heavily in its training program, called "Skill-ware." This training uses actual equipment rather than simulators and teaches basic, intermediate, and advanced word processing and spreadsheet packages, as well as data base functions and communications. Training may take from a half day to two days to complete. Exercises reflect activities an operator will encounter on the job. Skillware, which is currently available for fifteen soft-ware packages, has been translated into seven languages (French, Dutch, German, Danish, Norwegian, Spanish, and Hebrew) for use in the thirty-two foreign countries where Manpower has offices.

Much of the office automation training you will find in both national and independent temporary services is self-paced. This means you will be given a text and a machine, and you will guide yourself through a series of real-world exercises. At Debbie Temps in Niles, Illinois, temps can earn free personal computer training after 100 hours of working for them. Helene Kenyon of Debbie Temps explains, "We employ teachers on staff and teach two people per machine and ten hours per course. . . . We also have typewriters available to any temp who wants to practice and build speed and accuracy."

At our own service, Career Blazers, headquartered in New York City, we have taken the concept of training and developed it one step further. Career Blazers owns and operates a nationally accredited business school, offering instruction in a variety of business subjects. Our temps earn a free 20-hour course in any subject after 350 hours of employment. Most temps choose to take a personal computer curriculum which our school offers in seven software packages. Courses range from 10 hours to 300 hours in length; 100 percent financial aid is available to qualified participants. Often, we will pull our advanced students right out of the classroom and send them on an assignment. The sooner a temp can translate classroom theory to office applications, the quicker he or she will master the skill.

When you visit with several temporary services, ask them about their training programs *before* you register for employment. In addition:

1. Learn what the expected pay difference can be once you've completed training.
2. Ask if training is free, or if there is any employment commitment on your part in order to participate.
3. Find out exactly what kind of training is offered and compare that with the number of advertisements you see for this skill.

4. Ask to see where instruction is provided and in what form it is given—classroom, one-on-one, self-taught.

MARKETING TEMPS

Before we discuss the other three major areas of the temporary marketplace, we would like to call your attention to a classification of employees who, while they are not necessarily office temps, are generally provided by services in the office market or one of their divisions or subsidiaries. These temps perform marketing responsibilities. This is a very broad field and encompasses such occupations as:

- Sales Staff
- Telemarketers
- Pollsters
- Product Demonstrators
- Comparison Shoppers
- Convention Hosts and Hostesses
- Trade Show Support Staff, such as models, booth assistants, and registration aides
- Specialty Characters (i.e. Santa Claus, trademark figure)

Western Temporary Services of California is another of the major national temporary services. Western has several specialty divisions beyond the usual clerical and light industrial, one of which is Western Marketing Services. Western's versatile marketing team has hosted a trade show exhibit in London, portrayed costumed characters in a twenty-one-city toy promotion, made door-to-door surveys in twenty-five southern cities, introduced a ballpoint pen throughout Australia, distributed 350,000 coupon books a day in northern California supermarkets, and canvassed 2,000 video stores in four major cities to provide a new home video release.* You could even work as a fragrance or cosmetic model for Western Marketing Services.

Sound interesting? This may be a particularly good temporary employment choice for individuals who lack specific office skills but possess a friendly, outgoing demeanor, excellent communications skills, a good fashion image, and pleasant phone voice.

Jenny Zink, vice-president, national marketing division of Western Temporary Services, says this area of temping is equally popular with both men and women. "We look for sales-oriented individuals capable of working with the

---

*From Western Temporary Services Marketing Division brochure, reprinted by permission of Harvey L. Maslin, president, Western Temporary Services.

public." Zink stresses the importance of personality and grooming, and reports that her marketing temps go through required classroom training developed by Western. For example, Western has practically cornered the market on Santa Claus. They have a Santa Division which annually sends out 3,000 temporary Santas, each of whom has gone to Western's University of Santa Claus®. A Santa temp is given a thorough background check, views a video training program, and attends four hours of classroom lectures which include role-playing and a list of do's and don'ts regarding statements to children. Zink says that Western even maintains a wardrobe of 500 Santa suits, complete with wigs, beards, and belts. Santa temps are found at malls, building lobbies, retail stores, and office parties; they can expect to earn between $5.50 and $6.50 per hour.

According to Zink, Western's marketing clients range from retailer to manufacturer and even ad agencies, depending on the size of the promotion or campaign. She told us of a recent order. She had to fill a spot for a costumed character for a tour across the United States. "We had real tight specifications . . . the temp had to be four feet eleven inches with a size six shoe, and would be required to perform before an audience of children." Zink said the screening process can be more intense for marketing temps, and in some cases, it is "almost like an audition." She added, "Unlike an office temp, whom you can replace fairly easily, it is difficult to replace a marketing temp, especially if you have restrictions in size and so on and you need the person immediately."

So, if you can convincingly ho-ho-ho, or would like to handle an in-store demonstration of a new product, you might explore this aspect of tempting. Says Zink, "If you like working with people, it can be an interesting and often fun route to take." Zink does caution that not every temp service handles such assignments, and advises that it is most popular within large metropolitan areas.

INDUSTRIAL TEMPS

The biggest users of industrial temps are manufacturers. Little, if any, work experience is usually necessary for the many jobs in this market, which may include maintenance, warehousing, inventory taking, machine operating, collating, wrapping, packing, shipping, and trucking. Unfortunately, unskilled temporary laborers frequently receive much lower pay rates than regular employees in the same kinds of jobs. This is because the temporary service must cover the high costs of turnover prevalent among industrial temps. One assembly-line worker told us he had twenty-four jobs in three months.

Firms that utilize industrial temps frequently bring in this form of labor because their full-time workers burn out and become complacent about their repetitive jobs. An interesting study by the U.S. Bureau of Labor Statistics found that when an employee reports to work, he or she is considered to be 100 percent productive, and the probability for error is 0 percent. During the day, the percentage of productivity declines: At the end of an eight-hour day, the employee is 50 percent productive and his or her probability for error is 40 percent. The individual who is asked to work overtime may actually be doing his or her employer a disservice, since the eventual probability for error is greater than the individual's ability to be productive. Temps who are brought in to do repetitive tasks for short periods of time keep production levels steady.

A sampling of occupational titles in the temporary industrial market includes:

General Laborer	Security Guard
Janitor/Custodian	Shipping/Receiving Clerk
Maintenance Worker	Forklift Operator
Assembler-Mechanical	Inventory Clerk
Assembler-Electronic	Bottler
Quality Control Inspector	Solderer
Stock Handler	Loader/Unloader
Packer/Sorter	Trucker

The demand for industrial temps is both seasonal and cyclical. Few workers in industrial occupations are full-time temps, and the field is dominated by males.

MEDICAL TEMPS

Originally, temporary help firms created medical divisions to provide health-care personnel for institutions. This changed in the 1980s, when institutions began revising policy and made efforts to reduce hospital stays and increase outpatient services. In addition, as the population aged (people are now living longer), there emerged a need for long-term medical care, which created opportunities in home health care. Future increases in the field of medical temporaries are expected to concentrate in nursing homes and private residences.

Users in the medical market include hospitals, clinics, insurance companies, laboratories, private practices, and individual households. Hospitals, like most businesses, are adopting a lean staffing strategy and use temporary help to support a core of permanent employees. A major factor in the demand for temporary hospital personnel is the fluctuating patient population, which varies on a day-to-day basis. An occupied bed requires specific staff services. A low bed count represents lost revenue to the hospital, and it must adjust its payroll accordingly. Those occupations most affected include nurses, house-keepers, and food-service workers.

The trend toward reduced hospital stays began when the government (Medicare/Medicaid) changed payment policies on specific patient treatments. It will now pay only for a predetermined number of days for each procedure. Consequently, hospitals are discharging patients earlier, and thus people are recovering from surgery, strokes, and other medical conditions in convalescent centers and private homes. A nurse in the home substitutes for a nurse in the hospital. Nurses may supervise such care as intravenous therapy, medication, and respirator support.

Temporary Nurses

The U.S. Department of Health and Human Services predicts that by 1990 there will be a 40 percent shortage of nurses. While hospitals use temporary nurses to supplement their own staff, even medical temporary help firms are expected to feel the pinch.

In the early 1980s many nurses were put out of work by diagnosis related groups (DRGs). The DRG system allows a hospital to receive a fixed payment for a medical procedure, regardless of whether the hospital's cost is greater or less than the payment itself. This system is used by the government to reimburse hospitals for the care given to Medicare subscribers. Hospitals reduced patient stays to curb loses, and one area of cutbacks was the nursing staff. Now, just a few years later, frightened by the shortage, hospitals are trying to entice these same nurses back into their employ. In the interim, enrollments in nursing schools have dropped, and many nurses have moved into other areas of business and health care that pay higher wages and offer better working conditions.

Joel A. Klarreich, executive vice-president of Cosmopolitan Care Corporation, a regional medical temporary help service, says, "In New York City and all over, there is a critical shortage of skilled nurses. Recruitment is a real problem. . . . RNs can pick and choose the type of employment they want." Klarreich feels the shortage may be an outgrowth of the women's movment: "Nursing is not the profession of choice now. Other career opportunities are open to women who may have chosen to be an RN previously."

Home Health Care

Primary users in this field are families who need health care for a family member. In general, however, the family doesn't pay; rather, the paying client is the insurance company or government (Medicare/Medicaid). This type of care is usually set up indirectly through hospital discharge planners, physicians, and social workers. It can sometimes be difficult for a temporary service to locate the appropriate source of payment, and those being reimbursed by Medicare or Medicaid must be certified to receive such payments. Home health-care users are different from most customers of a temporary help firm because they are often one-time users which translates into little repeat business. Specific examples of this type of temporary assignment include assisting a patient who is recovering from surgery; caring for a terminally ill person; helping a new mother with baby care; caring for a patient with a condition such as kidney dialysis; and working with a stroke victim.

Two widely used categories of home health-care occupations are the companion and the home health-care aide. Typical assignments include custodial patient care through a terminal illness or caring for an elderly person. A home companion can help an elderly, handicapped, or recovering patient with housecleaning, cooking, and general errands. A home health-care aide has had previous training, either from the temporary service which employs him or her, or from a school or prior work experience; many have participated in certificate programs. Most private household assignments are long-term, that is, meaning two months or longer. All individuals who work for a health-care service are usually given a thorough screening, have had their professional licenses checked, and undergo a health examination.

Occupational titles in the medical temporary area include:

Registered nurse	Attendants
Licensed practical Nurse	Orderlies
Nurses aides	Home health-care aide
Medical assistant	Companion
Dietician	Medical secretaries
Laboratory technician	Insurance processors
X-ray technicians	General institutional Support staff

Many medical temporary services include office support staff specific to a health-related setting. Molly Landon of Medical Society Personnel Service, in Washington, D.C., adds, "Medical temporary help is an area of the temporary employment field which is growing in leaps and bounds. . . . Unfortunately, the current AIDS scare has caused some clinical medical workers to transfer to medical clerical jobs."

TECHNICAL TEMPS

Traditionally, the temporary technical market has consisted of engineers, designers, drafters, and special technicians. Large-volume users have been and continue to be aerospace and electronics manufacturers, shipbuilders, automotive manufacturers, engineering firms, and other similar industries that depend heavily on defense work.

Within the technical temp sector, services supplying temporary employees are often called job shops. Job shops got their start in Detroit during World

War II. The automotive industry subcontracted work to crews of engineers and draftsmen through engineering services, which became known as job shops. Eventually, the shops evolved into personnel services and began exploring other avenues of technical expertise. Today, firms offering temporary technical personnel have upgraded the job shop image into highly specialized services with experienced, sophisticated technicians.

A sampling of occupational titles in the technical temporary help field includes

Artists	Architectural engineers
Technical illustrators	Industrial engineers
Drafters	Computer programmers
Electronic engineers	CAD operators
Chemical engineers	Field technicians
Civil engineers	Engineering Technicians
Quality control inspectors	Customer service technicians

How are technical temps used?

- To write manuals
- To design defense systems
- To produce tools and machinery
- To create software packages
- To build structures

The majority of temps in this area work on small to large contracts that are held by the customer hiring the temp. Many of these are government contracts. Technical temps are rarely used as fill-ins for vacationing or ill employees; instead, they work for an average of six months or longer on one project. Technical temps can often earn more money in temporary spots than they can in regular full-time jobs; however, few are covered for health insurance and fringe benefits like vacation or holiday pay. Some temps work in their local market, while others may relocate to another part of the country for the duration of the assignment. Technical Aid Corporation, in Newton Upper Falls, Massachusetts, has developed parallel companies in three major technical disciplines: technical personnel, EDP/MIS contractors (EDP/MIS is the common acronym for electronic data processing/management information system), and systems and programming applications. Anthony Balsamo, corporate vice-president, says, "Our temps can earn twenty to forty percent more income . . . one of our professionals can earn a year's salary in approximately nine months."

"These temps are building nuclear power plants, army tanks, cars, airplanes, moon-shot systems, and more," says one temp service representative.

According to the *Occupational Outlook Quarterly* (Fall 1986), prospects for technical temps look good through 1990:

> *A large part of the growth in these jobs is expected to result from increased investment in capital equipment. An investment boom is projected because of expected lower real estate rates, the prospect of a stable economy, and the desire of manufacturers to take advantage of new technologies, purchases of which were postponed during the low investment years from 1980 through 1982. Growth is also expected in defense-related industries.*

PROFESSIONAL TEMPS

Beyond the understood technical occupational titles, there exists a group of professionals, such as doctors, lawyers, and accountants, who fall into the technical category; however, because we found this to be a growing number of individuals with special skills, we've chosen to focus on them in Chapter 3.

Chapter 3

PROFESSIONALS—A NEW BREED OF TEMP

Imagine meeting the following people:

> A software writer for IBM.
> An emergency-room physician in Kansas.
> A tax accountant at a *Fortune* 100 giant.
> An attorney handling a lawsuit in Denver.
> A missile engineer for Lockheed.
> An architect in St. Louis.

What do these people share? A place on the temporary payroll. They are all high-level workers who have left the safety of steady jobs for a freer, perhaps more romantic, life-style. Although they represent a small percentage of the working population, they do signify the arrival of new attitudes and social change in the American workforce.

Each professional temp has his or her own story—the chemist whose first love is tournament bridge, the physician who is a concert cellist, and the attorney who won't give up her family for a corner office with a view at a top-tier law firm. They are making a statement: *It is okay to make your career fit around your life, rather than your life around your career.* And corporate America is paying attention.

Labor experts tell us that the rise of the professional temp is due largely to the change from an industry-based economy to a service-based economy. Individuals are able to market themselves and their talents with considerable ease. Companies say it is cheaper to pay for a specialized skill only as long as it is needed, and many feel it is strategically smart to use contract help when a business is growing extremely rapidly or is in a phase of uncertainty.

Professional temps have had a dramatic impact on the temp industry in general, upscaling its image and calling attention to the pleasures of temping as well as to the economic sense of using temps. One programmer told us, "I am financially and emotionally secure. . . . I never needed to be a company man." Most recently, the type of professions getting press include medicine, law, engineering, accounting, science, and management. Temp firms based on these specializations have been created, and the field is growing wider and wider. American universities graduate 37,000 laywers, 16,000 doctors, and 51,000 accountants annually; a growing number of these individuals will opt for temporary employment.

DOCTORS: LOCUM TENENS

Locum tenens is the Latin name commonly given to temporary physicians. The term means "placeholder" or "one who stands in for another." KRŌN Medical Corporation in Chapel Hill, North Carolina, pioneered the practice and contracted locum tenens jobs to more than 475 physicians in 1986. Dr. Alan Kronhaus, president and chief executive officer of the company is generally credited with its origin, having first offered the service in 1980. Today, the field is composed of approximately a half-dozen similar services. Kronhaus explains that he conceived the service for the rural physician (as Kronhaus was) who had difficulty arranging coverage for vacations, personal time, and in-service education. The idea took shape and grew. Now, in addition to rural practices, principal users include hospitals, clinics, medical groups, teaching hospitals, and private practitioners. "Other uses just grew out of the service. . . . The broad applications became apparent as we went along," says Kronhaus.

"Medicine is a traditionally conservative area, but acceptance of this idea is getting better. . . . We've just scratched the surface," says Kronhaus. This small area of temporary personnel is already a $50-million industry.

John Smith, executive vice-president at Locum Tenens, Inc. in Atlanta, Georgia, reports that "any medical setting may be a user of locum tenens coverage." User needs may include replacement for an ill physician, personnel coverage during the breakup or startup of a practice, hospitals in places with seasonal differences in population, interim coverage while a physician seeks a partner (the search usually takes four to twelve months), and institutions in the process of recruiting staff.

Doctors who pursue locum tenens work generally fall into five categories.

1. *The young doctor just out of residency.* An individual who isn't sure what he/she wants to practice or where. He or she may have been dissatisfied

during residency and now wants their next experience to be a trial period before commitment.

2. *The 50 + -year-old who is entering a period of life when the or she wants to slow down and phase out his or her practice* (this person may be both a client and a locum tenens). Someone who wants to travel and pursue other pleasures, yet wants to keep a hand in medicine.

3. *The in-between doctor.* Someone who is between jobs or in the period between residency and fellowship.

4. *The freedom seeker.* This group includes doctors who may want to work thirty-six weeks out of the year and spend the rest of the time traveling or making a hobby more of a reality. This is the doctor who prefers freedom and its rewards to a big paycheck.

5. *The part-timer.* Individuals who have more than one main career interest, for example, the doctor who teaches at a university, yet wants to continue to practice.

At KRŌN, over 80 percent of the locum tenentes make their association with KRŌN their only work. Many of the locum tenens firms offer three- to nine-month contracts with their employees. KRŌN currently guarantees a qualified family physician an income of $50,000 for working nine months, whether work is available or not. We checked with Locum Tenens, Inc.; Physicians Relief Network in New Braunfels, Texas; and Comprehensive Health Systems, Inc., in Salt Lake City, Utah. All reported that most temporary doctors are paid about what they would get starting out in group practices; this can range anywhere from $60,000 to $135,000 a year, depending on both a doctor's specialty and what fraction of a fifty-week year is actually worked.

To become a locum tenens, a physician will need to complete an application packet available from all the services in the field. Questions will include training, references, state licenses, and documentation of malpractice experience. Before signing up with a service, a doctor should find out how its malpractice insurance is written, for how much, by whom, and whether or not it includes coverage to protect the doctor should his or her association with the locum tenens firm end. The services pay for a doctor's transportation, temporary housing, malpractice insurance, and licensing fees for each new state. A doctor may register with as many of the services as he or she wishes. Most advertise in medical periodicals, and all have toll-free numbers.

LAWYERS

A handful of firms across the country have taken the term "temporary" and applied it to the legal community. The Lawsmiths, founded in San Francisco in 1985 by principals Robert Webster and Eric Walker, is one such service, and its success is spawning other similar services. "Law firms and corporate legal departments had an initial reluctance to the concept, but acceptance is rapidly spreading. Once they understand what we offer, the service speaks for itself," says Webster. Users, such as law firms, corporate counsel, and sole practitioners, turn to an attorney temporary service for a variety of reasons: research, law and motion appearances, depositions, and trial preparation, to name a few. "There is no typical assignment," says Webster. "They can range from a half-day appearance in court to massive litigation which may take many months to a year."

Robert Weiner, president of Law/temps which is based in Northfield, Illinois (a suburb of Chicago), tells us: "The idea of using attorneys on a temporary basis isn't new. Traditionally, when law firms needed supplemental lawyers, they would call up someone they knew; that's what changed—it has gone from the informal to the formal within a commercial context."

Attorney Andrew R. Jarett (now a principal at Law/temps) temped for two years prior to joining the firm permanently. "Getting started in my own practice was very difficult because it is so highly competitive in the Chicago area. I needed to work to earn money and fill gaps in time while I was trying to establish myself, so I started to temp. . . . It gave me the flexibility I needed." Temping opened Jarett's eyes to the opportunities available to a temporary service with an attorney specialty. He saw there was both a need and a ready supply of potential temps. "We can fill a need, especially for small firms, and sole practitioners," says Jarett. "We can help their practices survive and expand." Is practicing law as a temporary attorney a positive experience? Jarett says yes. "Temping gave me great learning experiences. . . . I got advice on new ways to expedite work and could test it out. . . . I was able to explore and practice different types of law." Others in the field tell us there are some drawbacks. By being a temporary, an attorney rarely gets the personal satisfaction of seeing a case through to the end, and some individuals miss the sustained client contact. Further, attorneys tend to be "status conscious." One temp, now a permanent associate, told us, "You may feel as though you are being condescended to. . . . You are often judged by the firm you work for." Critics are concerned over the possibility of conflicts of interest when temporary attorneys have access to a wide variety of cases and firms. Still, the industry seems to be growing despite its flaws.

At the Lawsmiths, the service maintains a portfolio of over 150 attorneys. Ninety percent of its lawyers have had three or more years in practice; over half, six or more years, and nearly a third, over a decade of experience. (The Lawsmiths does not deal in paralegals, recent graduates, or researchers.) Temporary attorneys include independent individuals seeking new freedoms rather than the partnership track, women with families, lawyers in between permanent positions, and sole practitioners with cyclical business (in slow periods they may temp and in busy periods they may be the user). "The majority of our temps are motivated by the quality of their life rather than by big bucks," says Webster.

All the services in this field appear to offer in-depth screening and verification of credentials. An attorney will be sent to a firm, and the firm then interviews the temporary themselves for quality control. The major time-saver is having a roster of attorneys with various kinds of legal expertise at a firm's fingertips. Firms are charged an hourly rate, which is negotiated prior to the beginning of an assignment. The temps can earn as much as $75 per hour. Most services say an attorney's earnings can be comparable to an associate's salary or more, depending on the individual's area of specialization and experience.

Robert Webster of The Lawsmiths predicts, "The future of our area of the industry looks good. . . . It will become more and more economically desirable. Firms cannot add associates every year when business doesn't justify it."

INDIAN CHIEFS

Not really, but that's how we've chosen to categorize the potpourri of professionals who make up this remaining area of temps. With a little bit of investigating, you can find services in almost any major specialty. The following represents our findings in areas we felt to be of the greatest interest to our readers.

ACCOUNTANTS

User All companies, all fields—mom-and-pop shops to huge conglomerates
Typical temp CPA, degreed accountant, recent college graduate
Typical assignment three to four weeks long. Fill in for vacationing or ill executives; work on special projects; handle budgets; audits, financial reviews, loan solicitation
Industry comment Stan Newmark, vice-president, Accountemps, a division of Robert Half of New York, Inc.:
  "Eighty percent of our people are seeking a permanent position."
Newmark also described his firm's "Executive Corner":
  It was an idea born out of the need that arises when a key executive is out of work for a lengthy period of time due to a serious problem. You can't replace the individual, but you do need someone in their place. . . . We provide management all the way up to a temporary chief financial officer or CEO.

SCIENTISTS

User High-technology firms, biotechnology firms, environmental firms, laboratories, chemical manufacturers, oil refineries, drug companies
Typical temp Recent graduate, experienced chemist, experienced scientist, Ph.D.

Typical assignment Four months plus. Handle backlogged samples, expert-witness testimony, lab tests, equipment selection, safety program setup, special projects

Industry comment Bruce Culver, president, Lab Support, Woodland Hills, California:

> *Our contractor data base grows significantly each week. More and more labs are using temps to maximize operational efficiency or to evaluate prospective new hires.*

PHARMACISTS

User Hospitals, pharmacies, corporations, retail settings

Typical temp Doctors of pharmacy (background can vary from nuclear pharmacist to nursing home consultant)

Typical assignment Fill in for vacationing or ill pharmacists or those on their regular days off; emergency relief

Industry comment Ronald Cameron, president, Cameron & Company, Rolling Hills Estates, California:

> *We've been doing this for nineteen years; and now, more and more managers are becoming aware of their payroll costs; temporary pharmacists are a cost-effective answer for many businesses. . . . We've also seen a higher level of interest, most recently from women in the field.*

CHILD-CARE PROVIDERS*

User Day-care centers: church centers, major child-care chains, small centers, hotels in high tourism areas

Typical temp High school and college graduates, retirees, former teachers, child-care employees, education majors

Typical assignment One day or more fill-in for ill or vacationing staff; provide care for children under school age

Industry comment Nita Ekwurzel, director of Special Projects, Community Coordinated Child Care/Teachers on Temporary Service, Orlando, Florida:

> *At peak times we are sending out twenty to thirty teachers per day. . . . Our problem is recruiting enough people—the centers hire our temps away. We have found the market to be very receptive, but we can't fill all our orders due to the shortage of teachers. Screening is essential. . . . We follow state regulations and perform our own checks; we also do training.*

---

*Child care has been included more for its innovative value as a new segment of temporary help.

COMPUTER INDUSTRY SPECIALISTS

User Corporations, government, banks/finance, education, hi-tech
Typical temp Minimum three years of professional experience—software engineers, programmers, technicians, EDP specialists, analysts
Typical assignment Varies; typical length three-plus months
Industry comment Tony Marolda, area vice-presient, EDP/Temps, Needham Heights, Massachusetts:

> *Many people after working two to three years want to stay technical and want to avoid management. Contract work gives them the opportunity to work on different state-of-the-art technology*

GENERAL

General designates services that do temporary contracting in several areas, such as software engineering, management consulting, manufacturing, and research and development.
User Banking, communications, manufacturing, computer/data processing, equipment, government, education, financial, marketing, and so forth
Typical temp Experienced professionals in specific industries
Typical assignment Varies in scope depending on field, most assignments three-plus months
Industry comment Alan Skvirsky, president, Rent-A-Consultant, Washington, D.C.:

> *We have between 4,000 and 5,000 people registered with us. There are many people who want to work for different companies and do what they really like to do. . . . You can be good at what you do, but not like to market yourself or pursue employment or even collect payment. . . . As a service we can do this for them. . . . The field is growing because both companies and the government are moving in the direction of hiring specialized professionals on an as-needed basis. It is economically sound.*

FINDING A SERVICE

Locating a service for your special talents is not as difficult as it may seem. First, many services are based in a certain area, but they send temporaries out on contracts and assignments all over the country. You can register with a firm in Indianapolis and work in Seattle or, of course, closer to home. Second, almost every service we interviewed was in the Yellow Pages, not necessarily with other temporary services, but sometimes listed under its specialty. For example, depending on where you live, a legal temporary service might be found under "Legal" or "Law." Third, most of the professional temps we spoke with had hooked up with their firms through a referral by a friend, business contact, or professional association. This was, by far, the most popular way of finding a service that they were happy with.

Services also run recruitment ads in newspapers and trade journals. Many run open houses and invite prospects to come in with their résumé for an interview. A few firms recruited through direct mail, using mailing lists of members of industry trade groups and associations.

THE PROS AND CONS

Many of the temps we spoke with in the professional marketplace loved their lives and temped as a career; they were neither seeking jobs nor pursuing outside passions. An overwhelming number had found that this career life-style was a way to focus on the aspects of their professions that they enjoyed the most without dealing with corporate politics or feeling guilty about not wanting to move up the expected ladders. These people always had work when they wanted it, with the exception of the creative group. In an attempt to see the big picture, we asked what the real problems were in choosing this way of life. We were told that some of the permanent staff on jobs where temps were working were not receptive, and insisted on checking over work until the individual either said something or proved his or her expertise. Several remarked that continually having to prove oneself was tiring, and some missed the advice and protection of a mentor. Those who had temped and then went back into permanent work (or attempted to) said that once outside the walls of the traditional work force, it was difficult to get back in. Employers were not skeptical of their skills but of their staying power—there was the perception that such a candidate had been out on his or her own and could leave again.

Finally, whether it truly is the jargon, or temporary professionals are more career- and status-conscious than they think they are, we found that almost all those in this category referred to themselves or their employees as freelancers, consultants, or independents. Rarely did we hear the term *temp*, although the way in which the services worked was, in fact, the way a temporary help service operates.

Chapter **4**

YOU AND YOUR SERVICE

The key to happiness in your life as a temp is building a good relationship with your temporary service. It's a partnership. The temporary service needs you to make it look good to its client company, and you need your temporary service to keep you busy when you want to work. But finding the right service isn't as easy as closing your eyes and sticking a pin in the Yellow Pages. Different services have different personalities, and you owe it to yourself to be finicky. Shop around and see what's out there before you make your decision. Right now, temporary help firms are begging for people. They have more orders than they can fill, and a good temporary employee is a highly marketable commodity.

CHOOSING A SERVICE

Give the same time and consideration to finding a temporary employer as you would a permanent one. After all, it will be your new "boss." There are over 7,000 services nationwide, and they not only have different corporate personalities but they also serve vastly different markets. If you are a secretary, you do not want to waste time talking to services that specialize in warehouse personnel. There are national firms that have branches or franchises around the country. Names that might be familiar to you include Kelly, Olsten, Manpower, Adia, Western, and Norrell. There are also large privately owned firms with multiple offices, and there are smaller local services whose owners may operate at a single location or several in nearby areas.

1. *Make a list of possible services.*

- Check out your Sunday paper; look in the recruitment classifieds under Temporary Help. What do you see? Many of the ads share common denominators: the use of terms such as "high rates," "long- and short-term assignments," "bonuses," "free training," and "great benefits." Most ads indicate their area of speciality, e.g., word processing or industrial. Some newspapers have separate sections for temporary services, and they may not be listed alphabetically. Also be sure to check headings of skill areas (such as customer service, paralegal, or programmer).

- Look in the phone book. Surprise! You will *not* find prospect firms under "Temporary Services." Instead, look under the heading "Employment Contractors—Temporary Help." Review the ads in Figure 1. Which ones appeal to you?

- Ask your friends for recommendations; the best way to find a quality service is always through a referral. If you know someone whose firm hires temporary help, find out which service(s) the firm uses. Is the firm happy with that service?

Hint: If you will be using temporary employment in order to obtain a permanent position, review the "Employment Agency" section of the classified ads and telephone directory. Pay attention to which agencies also operate temporary services: Working with one of them might expedite your search and make your parting, once you find what you are looking for, a little bit easier.

Did you review what the ads in our sampling say? How do they compare with the ads in your newspaper? Notice how they target special audiences and skills. Be sure you've taken an inventory of your own current skills; then you can target your services.

2. *Call your prospects.* Many temps omit this step, and it is a mistake to do so. Call the service even if their ads indicate that no appointment is necessary. How are you treated? This is an all-important clue to how you will be treated forever after. Once a service meets you and begins sending you on assignments, your only contact with them may be by telephone. So pay attention. Are they courteous, efficient, friendly?

Hint: During your call, ask when payday is. Why? Payday is *not* a good day to interview with a prospective service; it is usually very hectic. However, it *is* a great day to do some detective work. Visit their offices, even if it's only to pick up their literature. Go around noontime. As their temps arrive to pick up their checks, notice how they look. You should consider them your coworkers. Even though you may never share an assignment, you do share a service. The apperance and attitude of a service's temps say a lot about the service. You might even ask one or two if they like working with the firm.

3. *Do your homework.* In every market there is a need. You learn this need by reading classified advertisements and the business section of your largest

Figure 1. Sample newspaper ads for temp jobs.

local daily paper. Local industry will dictate what types of positions are most in demand. For example, a university town often requires an abundance of clerical help, particularly data processing; a high-tech area has a need for technical professionals; and a community with a large health-care facility may need a steady supply of medical temps.

How do your current skills compare with what is in demand? Take a personal inventory of your talents. What do you qualify for? This is an area many temps neglect. You can't go to a service and expect miracles. For instance, if you are looking for office assignments, don't expect $10 an hour if you type with two fingers. Expect to be paid what your skills are worth.

Hint: We encourage you to be open-minded about clerical assignments. We meet many people, particularly recent college graduates, who have a snobbish attitude about typing. It has been our experience that this is a foolish tack to take, especially if you are looking for a permanent job at a hard-to-get-into employer or in a glamor industry (advertising, publishing, television, public relations, and so forth). Competition is heavy for top companies, and just getting in is half the battle. Why not accept something to get your foot in the door, rather than hold out for a dream assignment that may never come? Our advice is never to be ashamed to admit you can type; in this era of the keyboard, it is an asset rathern than a hindrance.

After you have determined the market's greatest needs and how you meet these needs, verbalize—out loud—why you want to temp and what fields interest you. Practice this in front of a mirror. Be able to answer (1) why you want to temp; (2) what your ideal assignment would be; (3) how long you plan to temp; and (4) any special preferences you may have (e.g., no work on Mondays or long-term assignments only). Your personal interview with the temp service is going to be critical in determining where they will send you. If you are articulate and appear to have a sense of self, you will gain the service's confidence earlier than most temps.

4. *Visit the offices of at least four prospective services.* Most temporary services are situated fairly close to each other. In suburban locations, this can be near industrial parks, in corporate clusters, or in shopping centers. In major cities, sometimes ten or more services are in one building alone.

When you go in, apprise the office environment. Is it neat and attractive? Do workers appear to be busy? How are you greeted? Chemistry between you and the service is important if you are to have a good working relationship. Be comfortable with the people and your surroundings.

Hint: If you live in suburbia, with easy access to a large metropolitan area, you may want to visit temp services in both locations. Big-city pay rates are usually significantly higher than their suburban counterparts; but, of course, you will need to keep in mind the cost and length of the commute. It is also possible to work with a service that has offices in both locations. You can make yourself available to either location; and the hours you accrue will be cumulative, so you won't jeopardize any benefits. Some temps find this is a good way to blend the excitement and pace of the city with the convenience and relaxed atmosphere of the suburbs.

Hint: Consider registering for employment with both a national organization and a small, local, privately owned service. The national service may offer better benefits to its temps, but a smaller service may be more sensitive to local market conditions. The smaller service may also have a greater ability to be flexible about rates, and both clients and temps may find themselves treated with greater care. In other words, you may be more important to the local owner than to the national service. (They key word here is *may;* this is in no way a fact, but an observation.)

Be sure you are dressed professionally for your visit regardless of the area of temporary employment you are entering. This is an interview. Dress conservatively. Women should wear a suit or a dress with a jacket; men should wear a suit or a jacket and tie. Don't stop in to investigate the service in casual clothes such as jeans. And go alone. This may sound like common sense, but too many potential temps show up with toddlers in tow.

5. *The best time to visit a temp service is Monday at 10 A.M. or Friday at 3 P.M.* Why? These are the busiest hours for a temp service and offer a temp the best opportunity to get an assignment. If you arrive too early on a Monday, you will get lost in the confusion; but 10 A.M. is just about right. It is after the initial chaos but exactly the time when a service may still be trying to find a replacement for a temp who didn't show, and it is also the time when a service is trying to fill any open orders that have just come in for the day or week. If you happen to be dressed appropriately and your skills match a need, you may find yourself on an assignment immediately. Likewise, Friday is also a good day because a temp service is trying to fill its open orders for Monday.

6. *Be prepared to spend time filling out an application and taking tests.* Allow yourself up to an hour and a half per visit. Some of this time will be spent filling out forms, taking tests, waiting to be seen, interviewing. Having a resume with you rarely precludes you from completing forms, or exempts you from test-taking. Have names and phone numbers of references with you. Write legibly, and answer questions honestly. Don't balk at taking tests, even if you are insulted by their content. Tests may include a general aptitude assessment, English usage, mathematics, or exercises designed to test your knowledge in a special area, for example, a digesting test for paralegal temps or a hands-on equipment test for PC operators. The tests are likely to vary from service to service; but don't be surprised if some are the same, particularly those that assess office automation skills. There is an effort in the industry to standardize skill assessment, and some testing organizations have created sophisticated exercises to measure operator knowledge. These tests are being marketed and sold specifically to the temporary employment industry.

Remember, oblige the service and take its tests. The service is not trying to screen out as much as it is trying to assess your current skills and their ability to place you on varied assignments. A sevice must be able to keep quality control checks on its employees, especially since they cannot actually see your on-the-job performance on a daily basis the way most employers can.

In addition, complete the employment application, even if you've brought a resume with you which provides all the information the service is asking for. A résumé is an excellent outline to be used during your personal interview, but the service will use the employment application for permanent record-keeping.

7. *Bring documentation to support your employment eligibility.* Have you heard about the Immigration Reform and Control Act of 1986? The act holds two important provisions for employers:

- Employers are prohibited from knowingly hiring illegal aliens. This requires employers to verify that a prospective employee is eligible to work in the United States by complying with the Employment Verification System.
- Employers may not refuse to hire or discharge an individual because of his or her national origin or citizenship status.

As your prospective employer, your temp service will ask you to complete an I-9 form created by the Immigration and Naturalization Service. Then the service will verify your eligibility to work after someone has examined the necessary documents you have provided. These documents include the following:

Any one document from this column:	OR	One document from the following two lists:
☐ A U.S. passport ☐ Certificate of U.S. citizenship ☐ Certificate of naturalization ☐ Unexpired foreign passport with attached Employment Authorization ☐ Alien Registration card with photograph		☐ A state-issued driver's license or ID card with photograph ☐ U.S. Military card *AND* ☐ Original Social Security card ☐ A birth certificate bearing an official seal ☐ An unexpired INS Employment Authorization form

Save yourself an extra trip and demonstrate your efficiency by bringing these items with you on your initial visit to a service. Every service must ask for them.

8. *Conduct yourself in a professional manner during your interview.* Your meeting with the temporary service representative is *very* important. Temp service personnel are trained to make quick judgments about your ability to do the job and represent them well to their clients. The person you meet with is usually the same person who will call you to send you on your assignments. Services may refer to this individual by any of the following names: assignment manager, temp manager, temp dispatcher, temp counselor, employee representative, and so on. In our writing, we will use the term assignment manager (AM). Most interviews take approximately twenty minutes, although professional/technical personnel may require an hour or more.

Shake hands firmly and smile. Your AM is already doing a quick check in his/her head as to what clients your own personal image is best suited for. Your AM will ask you why you are temping and what kind of work you are looking for. Here is where your practice pays off. Don't answer with an "I don't know"; instead, respond intelligently and firmly with an answer you have already given some thought to. Maintain eye contact when you are speaking, nod to show you understand, and don't fidget nervously.

What They'll Ask You

Here are some questions typically asked of prospective temps:

- *Have you ever temped before? If yes, for how long and with which service(s)? Did you like your assignments?*
- *If you've never temped before, do you understand how temping works?*
- *Why are you seeking temporary work?*
- *Do you have any time or scheduling restrictions?*
- *What are you looking for?*
- *Is there anything you specifically don't like to do?*
- *Are you prepared to take some skill assessments (tests) today?*
- *Where have you worked previously? What did you do?*
- *How late/early can I call you? Will you have any transportation problems?*
- *Can you give me the names of employers and/or personal references? Is there anyone else you can recommend to temp for us?*

Someone once said that the nicest part of temporary work is that there is generally no waiting. In other words, people at your temp service won't say, "We'll be making a hiring decision by Monday." Instead, they usually ask, "Can you start today or tomorrow?" In contrast to typical job interviews, you are rarely asked about your greatest achievement or what your strengths or weaknesses are. Temp services tend to hire on their perception of your ability to be reliable, responsible, to not do inappropriate things at a client's place of business and your overall appearance.

What to Ask Them

At a point when you feel the interview is near an end, ask the AM questions about working with their service. Your inquiries might include the following:

- *What kinds of assignments do you specialize in?*
- *Who are some of your major clients?*
- *What rate can I expect for my skills?* (The temp service will probably offer a range here. Ask what qualifies you for the high end of the range.)
- *Can your service keep me busy?*
- *What is the length of a typical assignment?*
- *Do you offer any skills training? If yes, is it free or will I have to pay for it?*
- *What is your vacation policy?*
- *Is there a medical and hospitalization plan? If so, how is coverage paid? Will it continue if I have a break in my assignments?*
- *Do I get paid for referring other temps?*
- *How and when am I paid? Are paychecks drawn from a local bank, or are they mailed from another city?* (This can affect how quickly your checks may be cashed.)
- *What is the policy if the business where I am working on assignment wants to hire me permanently?*
- *Can I expect seniority bonuses or merit raises for good job performance?*

What you find at your interview at a temporary employment service may be summarized on the form shown in Figure 2.

We recommend that you register with a minimum of two services: One to be your primary employer, the other as a backup to ensure that you are kept working. If your interview goes well, the service may ask you to wait a few minutes in their reception area so they can see if they have any assignments you can be set up for immediately. It is not unusual for a new temp to be unemployed on a Monday and working on a Tuesday. A good service *will* put you to work right away so that they won't lose you to the competition. If you don't hear from your new service after a day, call. In fact, most temp services say they *want* temps to call them. As one temporary industry staff member told us, "The squeaky wheel gets oiled . . . or the temp who keeps calling in gets the job."

BUILDING A RELATIONSHIP WITH YOUR SERVICE

A service needs to see how you perform at one or two assignments. That's why your first few weeks will be a trial period. During this period, try not to give your service a hard time, or your phone will quickly stop ringing. Let the

Figure 2.   Form for evaluating a temporary employment service.

Service name: _____

Address: _____

_____

Phone number: _____

How I heard of them: [   ] Referral   [   ] Newspaper Ad

[   ] Yellow Pages   [   ] Radio/TV   [   ] Other _____

Date(s) visited: _____

Whom I spoke/met with: _____

Tests taken: _____

Impression of the office: [   ] Busy   [   ] Friendly
[   ] Professional   [   ] Efficient   [   ] Courteous
[   ] Helpful   [   ] Rude   [   ] Slow
[   ] Unprofessional   [   ] Unpleasant

Benefits offered: _____

_____

Pay range quoted: _____

Assignment given: _____

Comments: _____

_____

_____

people at your service see you as a cooperative, professional employee; earn their respect and confidence. Like any new employee, you have to establish rapport.

You may get calls for assignments in the late evening or in the early morning. Let the service know how late they can reach you and how early. It is not unusual for an AM to wake his or her temps up and send them on a same-day assignment. Learn to expect this. Furthermore, get yourself a telephone answering machine if you don't already have one.

When you are offered an assignment, ask what it pays (not every assignment will be at the same rate) and ask about the client.

- What does the company do?
- What is the atmosphere like—conservative, casual, creative, and so forth?
- Is there anything special I need to know about the client?
- How do I get there, and whom do I report to?

Keep a pad and pencil near every phone in your home or apartment. Write the information down as you are speaking, especially if you are just waking up.

A Word About Attitude

While researching this book, we spent a considerable amount of time with our own temporary division asking questions and observing the staff in action. At one point, we asked what the biggest problem was in meeting and working with temps. In chorus, the group answered, "Attitude." "What about attitude?" we probed. "Don't have one" was the response.

If you want to get your relationship with your service off on the right foot, the best advice we can give you is to come in their doors dressed professionally, smile frequently, and stress your flexibility. In the course of one day, we were truly surprised to observe applicants with limp handshakes; people who wouldn't look the interviewer in the eye or speak audibly; and most annoying were those individuals who came in with the proverbial chip on their shoulder. A temporary help service *wants* to hire you—don't give it excuses not to. If you are openly hostile or just plain unhappy about the prospect of temporary work, maybe you should reconsider whether it is a path you want to take. If you decide to temp, be positive about it, since you can always walk away from it with minimal risk.

Some Tips From Assignment Managers

Who can better offer you advice than the people who will be sending you out on assignments? We asked the Career Blazers team for a list of things every AM's "Dream Temp" would do. Here's what they told us:

- Come in for an interview dressed in corporate attire.
- Accept calls as late as 11 P.M. and as early as 6 A.M. ("I remember last-minute favors and always pay back with a great assignment the next time.")
- Call in regularly if you are hard to reach.
- Get an answering machine, preferably one you can check in with by remote.
- Ask for details when you are given an assignment.
- Show up on an assignment. (The AM's nightmare is the no-show temp.)
- Call in when you arrive your first day on a new assignment.
- If you are forced to cancel an assignment you have already accepted, give your service as much notice as possible.
- If you have a problem at a client, call your service first. Let them decide what to do; let them be the heavy.
- Let your AM know if your assignment is continuing beyond the original date.

Accepting an Assignment

If you want to ensure that you are only called for those assignments you are likely to accept, tell your AM during the interview what your special preferences are. We have known a New York City legal secretary who will only work on Fifth, Madison, and Park avenues between 42 Street and 57 Street, a temp who will only work in publishing companies, and still another who is available for work only on Mondays and Tuesdays. All of these individuals made their requirements known up front, and their services have honored them. However, keep in mind that the more flexible you are, the greater your opportunities for employment.

Once you accept an assignment, it is your duty to let your service know if you cannot make it or complete it. If you get sick, don't call the client. Call your temp service—it is your employer. Most temp services open before 7 A.M. and close well after 5 P.M., and many maintain twenty-four-hour answering services.

When a service tells you an assignment is of indefinite length, it is usually asking for a minimum two-week commitment. Don't be afraid to say that two weeks is all you can do; once you've finished your two weeks, you can always agree to stay if the assignment is continuing. If you don't like what you're doing, you've already told your service you couldn't commit to anything longer, so you are safe either way.

Asking for and Receiving Favors

You won't regret becoming friends with your assignment manager. If possible, go in person to pick up your checks once in a while instead of always having them mailed to you. Enable your service to match your name to a face. Some temps never see the inside of their service after their initial interview.

If you go on vacation, send your AM a postcard or a Christmas card or birthday card. You want him or her to like you. Why? It often means better assignments and higher rates when he or she can be flexible.

Some temps report that they often feel pressured into taking an assignment. Or worse, they feel their service misrepresents the assignment just to get them to take it. We won't say this doesn't happen because we know it does. However, it is much harder to be pressured or cajoled by someone who thinks of you as a person, not just a phone number.

What are typical favors your service may ask of you?

To take on a "rotten assignment"—the client is difficult.

To take a lower rate than usual for an assignment, particularly one that doesn't make maximum use of your skills.

To accept a boring assignment.

To be at a client's place of business in less than an hour.

To work at a location that is hard to reach or off the beaten path.

What can you expect in return? Usually your assignment manager will ask you to do the service a favor, and will literally plead with you to accept the assignment. This is when you are in a position of power. Be honest; tell your AM you would love to help out even though the assignment doesn't sound very attractive. How can the AM help you out? Have something in mind: a specific industry for your next job, a better rate, or an easy assignment. Be warned: the AM may promise you anything and then forget—if you allow that. Don't allow yourself to be manipulated. Speak up. It's okay to remind your service of the favor you did. Just be pleasant, and don't make it sound as though you are holding it hostage.

Our favorite story is about one of our own temps. She came to us with her degree in journalism and had a burning desire to get into a newsroom. Sandy was asked to take on a difficult client, a woman known to be a "screamer." We warned Sandy about her and promised that the next order that came through at one of our area's prize-winning dailies was hers. A little over a month later we made good with our promise. We had an order that put her in the heart of the newsroom of a well-known newspaper, amid the craziness and frantic pace of editors and reporters. Originally, it was a three-day gofer spot; but Sandy loved it, and the paper loved her. She's now a permanent employee there. Says Sandy,

I hated every minute of that first assignment, and I called in every day and told my AM how awful it was. She kept telling me to hang in there, that she would have something good for me. I told her if she had the faith in me not to walk—and it was really a miserable job—then I had faith in

her to get me a publishing spot; but I never expected her to come through the way she did!

AT A CLIENT

Get to an assignment early. Not every client will be organized enough to greet you at the door and make you feel comfortable in your temporary surroundings. Some clients simply don't know how to handle this process efficiently. Ghenia Websterss, a PC operator, whom you may remember from the Introduction, related this experience to us:

I always arrive early because you never know how long it will take you to get where you are going. Today, for instance, my temp counselor gave me the wrong floor. I was on several floors before I found anyone who could help me. If you are assigned to a big company and you don't know where to go, ask for personnel or human resources . . . this is usually a good starting point. Anyway, personnel sent me to an entirely different building a few blocks away! Once I got there, I had even more trouble. They weren't sure where I was to report until I told them what I knew about the assignment. This whole thing took over thirty-five minutes. In a large company, a simple procedure like hiring a temp can get very confusing; but don't let it throw you.

Websterss, by the way, was a savvy temp. She got the names of the people she spoke with along the way (in case her excuse needed verification), and she apologized to the person she was reporting to and explained the delay. At the first available moment, she called her temp service to tell it what happened. It is best for you to keep your service informed of any problems so that it will not be surprised by a disgruntled client calling before you do.

Once you reach your destination, introduce yourself to those around you. Explain that you are a temp from XYZ Service and smile. Usually, one person will be assigned to show you what work is to be done and how to operate any special equipment. Beware. Some temps have told us that you shouldn't expect miracles, that you may find yourself in a sink-or-swim situation. We tell you this not to scare you but to prepare you. Be resourceful and don't panic. And if you don't know something, *ask*. Bring your own pad with you and take notes. Unfortunately, if you are temporarily replacing someone else, much of the information you will need in order to do the job properly is in the head of the regular person (to whom you rarely have access). So, be a problem-solver. Look for information in reasonable places, such as files, desk drawers, and storage cabinets near you. If you ask coworkers for information, write down their response so you won't have to ask a second or third time.

Some coworkers will welcome a temp; others will ignore you; and still others will go out of their way to be rude to you. A temp shoulders the blame or the

blessing for all the temps who have gone before him or her. If their last encounter was a positive experience, they are likely to be receptive. If not, we
think you can guess. Just be yourself and get the work done. Remember that
sooner or later the assignment will end.

Temps report that it is common to find either too much work for them to
complete or not enough work to keep them busy. If you are sure that the
workload is unreasonably heavy, let your service know. It may attempt to market another temp to the client. If you are enjoying your work, too much work
can be a good thing, because it can turn a one-day assignment into a one-week
assignment or longer. Too little work means you will have to look busy or ask
for more work to do. A temp in Phoenix tells us:

> I've sat at a desk where the phone never rang. I had a boss who gave me
> two letters to type the entire day. . . . I never saw him. My requests for
> more work were ignored. . . . I ended up reading a book. They really
> didn't need a temp. . . . I can't believe they even needed a full-time per-
> son in that position. I was getting paid eight dollars an hour to be some-
> one's secretary in name only. . . . I guess it was a status thing.

One widespread complaint from temps about their life-styles is the inability
to see a project through to completion. "I reorganized a firm's entire filing
system, but I don't know if they are following it," says Gail Scheurman, a temp
industry veteran. "If you like continuity, don't temp. . . . It's like reading a
mystery halfway through and never learning who the murderer is."

If you are on an assignment that has gone well, or if you have received a
compliment on your job performance, ask the client to tell your temp service.
Waiting passively for positive feedback won't make your temp service notice
you. You want to build some credibility with your service in order to ensure
that it will be responsive to your needs. Many services either send performance reports or make follow-up calls to a client to see how well you did.
Encourage your supervisors to cooperate by completing the form or taking the
call. Even better, if things have gone really well, ask them to write a letter to
your service (be sure you get a copy). Not only will your service love what
is being said about you but it makes a nice client testimonial for them, and
they are likely to show it off. Positive feedback will help you increase your paycheck and get the choicest assignments the service has to offer. We met
one temp who was her firm's "client-clincher" temp. Whenver they broke
into a new account, she was the temp they sent to represent them. As she
described it:

> I enjoy helping to sell the service, and they have rewarded me with bo-
> nuses and top rates. . . . Sometimes I even go on assignments where I
> don't use all of my skills . . . but they still pay me a high rate because
> they know I know how to make a client love me.

Use the form in Figure 3 to keep track of your assignments from varied services. We suggest that you monitor your temp activity so that you can easily remember which assignments you favored and where they originated from.

SENSITIVE ISSUES

While you are working as a temp, you may find that you are faced with issues that need to be handled with some sensitivity and good judgment. We list some of the concerns common to most temps. You may not encounter all of these situations, but there is a good chance that you will find yourself in one or two of them while you are temping.

You Hate Your Assignment

It happens. Once in a while you find yourself on the worst assignment imaginable. If you are having a difficult time, call you AM immediately. *Never, ever walk off an assignment.* It may be that you dislike your coworkers or the boss may be a screaming lunatic or you can't stand what you are doing or whatever. But remember, you made a commitment to your service. That doesn't mean you have to stick out an unbearable situation, but you do owe it to your service to let it know how you are feeling.

A temp dispatcher from Dallas told us:

I got a frantic call from a temp who said she was going nuts in her assignment. When I picked up the phone, the first thing she said to me was "Get me out of here." I was surprised because I had never had complaints about this client before, but this temp had a real problem with the woman she sat next to, who was a permanent employee. My temp agreed to finish the day, but wouldn't complete the assignment, which was scheduled for two more days. I tried to entice her with a higher rate, a bonus—anything; but she was adamant. So, I took her off. . . . I had to. She was a temp who had always cooperated and she had credibility with me. . . . She had a legitimate grievance.

So if you can't stand your assignment, tell your service; but use your judgment. Make sure the situation really is intolerable, because you don't want to get a reputation for "crying wolf." Also, services know that some temps try to extort higher rates from them by saying an assignment is awful. Save your SOS for serious situations. One of the best things about temping is knowing you won't be in a certain job forever—they do end!

Always let your service decide if the problem you have with an assignment is solvable. In some instances, a temp's concern may cause the service to terminate a relationship with a client. Never do anything you know is illegal or

Figure 3. Form for keeping track of assignments.

Start Date	End Date	Client Name	Service Name	Total Hours	Pay Rate	Skills Used	How Was It?

something you find unethical, even if the client requests it and says that's why you are there. When in doubt, call your service; it is the service's worry, not yours.

The Temp Working Next to You Earns More per Hour

First of all, it probably isn't the smartest thing to discuss your salary with a coworker. However, if you have discovered that you are receiving dissimilar rates for the same job, the most important question is, what service is the other temp working for? It could be that your coworker does not work for the same service you do. His or her employer may have decided to pay more because of the temp's seniority with the service or overall skills, or because the difference between what it is paying the temp and charging the client is less than the markup of your own service. First, be sure your coworker temp is telling you the facts. If you are reasonably sure that he or she is, call your AM and explain what you have discovered. The AM will probably want to know which service the other temp works for, how long he or she has been with them, whether this is the temp's usual rate, and whether the individual has any skills that you don't have, even if those skills are not being utilized in that particular job. Most services will match the rate but will preface it by stating that it is for this assignment only (especially if it is considerably higher). If the service doesn't match the rate, and perhaps even if it does, you may want to investigate what the competing service has to offer. Some temps switch services because the pay rate is the most important part of their decision to work with a particular service. That is something only you can decide.

You have a bigger problem if your higher-paid coworker is from your service. If you are both doing exactly the same work, you are probably working on a project. As a rule, services who send a number of temps to work on a project pay all the temps at the same rate. Again, ask your service to explain the discrepancy. The response should determine whether or not you will choose to continue to work with it. During our interviews with services, we learned that the only reasons services consider paying one person more is when the higher-paid temp has more work experience with the service and/or additional skills, or when the temp has agreed to take the assignment as a favor to the AM. Most services agree that they would rather have their temp ask about the rates than lose the temp without an opportunity to respond. If you don't communicate a problem, it can't be solved.

A Permanent Employee Wants to Know How Much You Earn

It is not usual for a temp to make more money per hour than a permanent employee. If an employee asks you about your rates, it is perfectly permissible to decline to answer; but do it pleasantly. You don't want to create any unnecessary animosity between you and the permanent staff. You might answer by saying, "Not nearly what I'm worth," or something equally safe. However, if you are pressured and feel you must respond, it is best to answer that you are paid a different hourly rate on every assignment and then give your range. If you know that the permanent employee is making less per hour, you might then ask if he or she has a benefits package, since many people neglect to include this in their annual compensation.

One temp told us that he deserved to make more than the permanent employees because he worked much harder and had a better understanding of the work than they did. Of course, he didn't want to tell them that, so he explained that he only worked a few days per week and was working at the highest rate his service would pay him so that he could make ends meet.

> *I felt uncomfortable, but I didn't want to live with their hostility. . . . I ended up making temporary work sound awful, even though I love it. Some people get threatened when they see a temp come in and do a good job. . . . I always take a low profile on my assignments. . . . I'm temping because I'm a writer; I'm not there to make friends or enemies.*

A Client Wants to Hire You Without Telling Your Service

Unfortunately, what is known in the industry as *pirating* does occur. What the client is trying to do is steal you away from the temporary service. It may present the offer like this: "The temp service is paying you $10 an hour and the service is charging us $14 an hour. Let's make us both happy: We'll pay you $12 an hour and we'll bypass the service."

Don't let such offers tempt you. And think twice about working for such a client. Companies who try to do this know it is against their contract, which is why they want to keep it quiet. If you really want to work there, tell the company it must go through your service. Some will oblige, and those that won't will probably terminate your assignment. Why don't they want your service to know? Because they have agreed to pay your service a charge known as *liquidated damages* to compensate the service for the loss of their employee. The amount of the liquidated damage varies from service to service. It is always the responsibility of the client to pay this charge. Do not let anyone tell you that you must contribute to it. Most services require a temp to tell them of a possible temporary-to-permanent conversion and outline this policy on the back of a temporary employee's time sheet. Be sure you read your service's time sheet when you sign it and submit it for your weekly wages.

Negotiating a Higher Rate

Asking for a raise can be a difficult experience. Hopefully, your service will have a policy that gives temps periodic raises for excellent job performance. However, let's assume you are working with a service that seems to ignore pay increases. You have two choices: You can register with another service or you can ask for a raise. If you have enjoyed your assignments and you work well with your AM, go for the raise. Of course, you will need to back up your request with proof that you are an asset to their staff. For example:

- Have you learned any new skills since you first signed up with it?
- Have you agreed to over 90 percent of the assignments you've been called for?
- Do you have a good record for being on time and not calling in sick?
- Has the service received letters or calls commending your abilities?
- Are you requested back by companies where you've worked?
- Do you look and act like a professional?
- Have you been with the service for at least six months?

If you can answer yes to these questions, we think your service will be agreeable to negotiation. Sometimes a service simply overlooks a temp's rate because its payroll is so large; sometimes a service is just being stingy and you need to call its attention to that fact. But before you ask for your raise, call other services and see what they pay for your skills. How do they compare? Get a fair figure in your head so you have a goal to work with. Then make an appointment to see your AM in person. Asking for a raise over the phone may be less stressful, but it also gives the service an edge: It can put you on hold or tell you it will call you back. A face-to-face confrontation is best.

Let us just clarify what we mean by "raise." We mean a raise at the *low* end of your rate. In other words, if you have been paid $13 to $15 an hour on various assignments, you want to increase your range by increasing the $13. Being told you can have the upper end of your range extended to $16 an hour for some assignments isn't as good as getting the $13 raised to $14.

The service should be able to tell you what kinds of skills they expect for a higher rate. Most temp managers recognize the value of a good temp, and you will get your raise. We must warn you, however, that you should always conduct yourself like a professional. Services frown on temps who "hold them hostage," for example, saying something like "I won't complete this assignment unless I get a raise." If you find your service takes a tough stand on the raise issue and you think you can get more somewhere else, then the decision is up to you to move to a new employer. Just as in a permanent position, sometimes you need a change of scenery to be appreciated.

SAMPLE FORMS AND HANDOUTS

The majority of temporary services create informational pieces for their temps. At Career Blazers, we give out *The Career Blazers Handbook* to all new temporary employees. The next few pages offer you a sample of our employment application and pages from the handbook (Figures 4–6). Although written for our own temps, our advice is so universal that it can be applied to all categories of temporary employees.

WHAT ABOUT BENEFITS?

Okay, let's imagine you are currently working as a temporary employee. What is the biggest drawback? Benefits. Or rather, lack of benefits, and temporary services know it.

More and more temporary services are implementing benefit programs in which their employees can participate, although most services require their temps to first accumulate a certain number of hours with their company. Temp services are instituting such plans in order to attract and keep people. "There's a definite shortage of temps," one service owner told us. "A large percentage of our job orders go unfilled due to the people shortage." Temporary help firms also lose their employees to permanent jobs, especially if the company to which a temp has been assigned has an excellent benefits package. This is an ironic twist, since the higher the level of benefit costs for permanent workers, the more likely a firm is to use temporary workers in order to keep personnel costs down.

If benefits are important to you, be selective about where you work. Before you register with a temporary service, ask about their benefits for temps— don't be shy! There are *no* set rules about benefits in this industry, but innovative services have implemented programs of varying scope. Almost all of the services we questioned based their benefits programs on accumulated temporary hours. When you visit, be sure to ask your prospective service these key questions:

1. *Are the hours that must be accumulated cumulative or consecutive?* For example, one service pays you one week of vacation after you've worked for that service 1,000 hours in any twelve-month period. Another will pay for a vacation after 900 hours of temp work, but the hours must have been accumulated for working consecutive 35-hour weeks.
2. *Do you begin accumulating earned hours from day one, or is there a calendar starting date?*
3. *Are health insurance benefits contributory, or are they fully paid by the service?*
4. *Are you automatically notified of your earned vacation, or must you monitor your hours yourself?*

Figure 4. Sample employment application from a temporary service.

CAREER BLAZERS TEMPORARY PERSONNEL

APPLICANT – PLEASE PRINT BOTH SIDES
COMPLETE ALL UNSHADED AREAS

DATE ___/___/___
    MO. DA. YR.

NAME _____ HOME PHONE (___) _____ S/S NO. ___/___/___
    LAST   FIRST   M.I.

ADDRESS _____ APT NO. _____ CITY _____ STATE _____ ZIP _____
ARE YOU SEEKING PERMANENT EMPLOYMENT ☐ YES ☐ NO
ARE YOU COLLECTING UNEMPLOYMENT BENEFITS ☐ YES ☐ NO HOW LONG? _____
AVAILABLE FOR WORK BEGINNING _____ UNTIL _____

AVAILABLE FULL DAYS: ☐ ALWAYS ☐ SOMETIMES ☐ NEVER
    EVENINGS: ☐ ALWAYS ☐ SOMETIMES ☐ NEVER
    WEEKENDS: ☐ ALWAYS ☐ SOMETIMES ☐ NEVER

WHY do you wish to work temporary? _____

DAYS AVAILABLE: ☐ MON ☐ TUE ☐ WED ☐ THUR ☐ FRI ☐ SAT ☐ SUN
HOURS AVAILABLE: ___to___ ___to___ ___to___ ___to___

ARE YOU PRESENTLY A STUDENT OR PLAN TO RETURN TO SCHOOL? ☐ YES ☐ NO ☐ MAYBE
HAVE YOU EVER BEEN BONDED? ☐ YES ☐ NO EVER BEEN REFUSED BOND? ☐ YES ☐ NO

OTHER PHONE (___) _____
MESSAGE PHONE (___) _____

I WILL USUALLY TRAVEL TO WORK BY ☐ PUBLIC TRANSPORTATION ☐ MY CAR
PUBLIC TRANSPORTATION CONVENIENT TO ME (LIST): _____
IN EMERGENCY, NOTIFY: NAME _____ ADDRESS _____ PHONE _____
HAVE YOU WORKED FOR OTHER TEMPORARY SERVICES? ☐ YES ☐ NO WHICH SERVICE(S) / WHEN? _____

HOW DID YOU HEAR OF CAREER BLAZERS TEMPORARY? ☐ FROM CAREER BLAZERS PERMANENT ☐ REPUTATION
☐ NEWSPAPER AD (NAME) _____ ☐ RADIO ☐ TV ☐ RECOMMENDATION BY _____
☐ YELLOW PAGES ☐ COLLEGE PLACEMENT ☐ POSTER–WHERE _____ ☐ FRIEND–NAME _____
☐ U.S. EMPLOYMENT SERV. ☐ OTHER _____

APPLICANT COMPLETE EMPLOYMENT AND EDUCATION RECORD

Most Recent First	COMPANY NAME / ADDRESS	NAME OF SUPV. TELEPHONE	TYPE OF CO. POSITION	SALARY START SALARY END	REASON FOR LEAVING
From:					
To:					
From:					
To:					
From:					
To:					

	Address	From	To	Grad./Degree	Avg.	Course of Study
High School						
College						
Graduate School						
Special School						

APPLICANT — CHECK BOXES INDICATING YOUR SKILLS AND EXPERIENCE

TYPING
☐ MANUAL
☐ ELECTRIC
☐ SELECTRIC
☐ EXEC W/O JUSTIFY
☐ EXEC W/JUSTIFY
☐ STATISTICAL
☐ MANUSCRIPT
☐ BILLING
☐ LEGAL
☐ TECHNICAL
☐ MEDICAL
☐ VARITYPE
☐ TRANSCRIPTION
☐ FOR. LANG.
☐ TELEX/TELETYPE

STENOGRAPHY
☐ PITMAN
☐ GREGG
☐ SPEEDWRITING
☐ STENOSCRIPT
☐ FAST LONGHAND
☐ FAST TYPEWRITER
☐ FOREIGN LANGUAGE ____
☐ STENOTYPE MACHINE
☐ MEDICAL
☐ LEGAL
☐ TECHNICAL
☐ OTHER ____

WORD PROCESSING
☐ MEMORY
☐ MAG CARD (MCST)
☐ I ☐ II ☐ A
☐ MAG TAPE (MTST)
☐ COMPOSER (MTSC)
☐ A B DICK
☐ AM JACQUARD
☐ BURROUGHS (REDACTRON) ___
☐ DEC
☐ IBM
☐ LANIER
☐ LEXITRON
☐ MICOM
☐ NBI
☐ QYX
☐ SAVIN
☐ VYDEC
☐ WANG
☐ WORDSTAR
☐ XEROX
☐ OTHER

SWITCHBOARD
☐ MONITOR BD MODEL ____
☐ PLUG BD MODEL ____
☐ CENTREX
☐ CALL DIRECTOR
☐ OTHER ____

BOOKKEEPING
☐ ACCOUNTS PAYABLE
☐ ACCOUNTS RECEIVABLE
☐ BANK RECONCILIATION
☐ GENERAL LEDGER
☐ TRIAL BALANCE
☐ PROFIT & LOSS
☐ PAYROLL
☐ PAYROLL TAXES
☐ CREDIT & COLLECTIONS
☐ COMPUTER BASED SYSTEM
  ☐ PREPARE DATA FOR INPUT
  ☐ COMPUTER OPERATOR
    SYSTEM/MODEL ____
☐ OTHER ____

DATA PROCESSING
☐ CRT
☐ KEYPUNCH NO. ____
  ☐ OWN PROGRAM
  ☐ VERIFIER
☐ INPUT/OUTPUT CONTROL
☐ COMPUTER OPERATOR
  MACHINES ____
☐ PROGRAMMER ____
☐ SYSTEMS ANALYST
☐ EDP SUPERVISOR
☐ OTHER ____

OFFICE MACHINES
☐ ADDER ☐ TOUCH
☐ CALCULATOR
☐ COMTOMETER
☐ BOOKKEEPING
  MODELS ____
☐ PITNEY BOWES
  MODELS ____
☐ MIMEO
☐ A B DICK
☐ MULTILITH DAVIDSON
  ☐ COLOR ☐ B & W
☐ COPIER
  MODELS ____
☐ DITTO
☐ OZALID
☐ MICROFILM/FICHE
☐ ADDRESSOGRAPH
☐ GRAPHOTYPE
☐ FOLDER
☐ OTHER ____

FOREIGN LANGUAGES
☐ READ ____
☐ WRITE ____
☐ SPEAK ____
☐ TRANSLATE ____
☐ INTERPRET ____

ADV/COMMUNICATIONS
☐ PROOFREADING
  ☐ WITH SYMBOLS
☐ EDITING
☐ COPYWRITING
☐ PASTE-UPS/MECHANICALS
☐ DESIGN–PRINT
☐ DESIGN–FASHION/TEXTILE
☐ RESEARCH
☐ PHOTOGRAPHY
☐ PUBLICITY/PROMOTION
☐ SALES
☐ MARKETING
☐ ILLUSTRATION
☐ FINE ARTS
☐ MEDIA ____
☐ OTHER ____

CLERICAL
☐ GENERAL
☐ COLLATING
☐ FILING
☐ FIGURE
☐ STATISTICAL
☐ INVENTORY
☐ RECEPTION
☐ MAILROOM
☐ SHIPPING/RECEIVING
☐ MESSENGER
☐ OTHER ____

Figure 5.   Sample handouts explaining employment agreement and rules.

Your Agreement with Career Blazers

Following is the agreement you signed when you completed your application:

I understand that Career Blazers' continuing ability to provide work for me and others desiring temporary work depends upon the quality of service received by clients. As an employee of Career Blazers, I therefore agree to comply with the following:

- I will be cheerful, courteous, professional and appropriately dressed on assignments.
- When I accept any assignment, I will report to work at the scheduled time every day until such assignment is completed.
- If, for any reason whatsoever, I must be absent or late in reporting for any assignment, I will notify Career Blazers at least two hours before the scheduled starting time. I understand that Career Blazers has a 24-hour telephone answering service.
- As soon as I know when an assignment is to terminate, I will notify Career Blazers. If I fail to do so, Career Blazers can assume that I am not available for further work.
- If any Career Blazers' client to whom I have been assigned offers me a permanent, temporary, or part-time job within 90 days of the end of such assignment, I will promptly notify Career Blazers and will not accept such offer beforehand.
- I understand that all matters relating to wages and rates are necessarily confidential and will never discuss same with clients or others.
- I will discuss any problems I have on assignments with Career Blazers, never clients.
- I authorize Career Blazers to check my references and educational history.
- To the best of my knowledge, all information given on this application is true. I understand that my failure to comply with any provision hereof may be cause for the termination, without notice, of my employment relationship with Career Blazers.

YOUR AGREEMENT

Keeping us Posted is Important

TELL US...

- when you are available for an assignment;
- when you've completed an assignment, even if you are not immediately available for a new one;
- if your assignment will be longer or shorter than originally specified;
- at least two hours in advance if you are going to be late or cannot make it to an assignment. DO NOT call the client—it is Career Blazers' responsibility to inform the client of your lateness or absence;
- if you will be working over 40 hours on a Monday-through-Sunday week;
- if you are asked to stay on indefinitely or permanently;
- if you are having a problem of any kind while on assignment;
- if you are being asked to use more of your skills than originally specified;
- if your skills are not suitable for your assignment, or your assignment is not suited to your skills;
- if you learn new skills or improve old ones;
- if you suffer an injury while on assignment;
- if there is a change in your name, address, phone number or tax status;
- if you know other qualified people seeking temporary or permanent work.

Reprinted by permission. © 1988 Career Blazers. May not be reproduced in whole or in part without the express written permission of Career Blazers.

5. *Can you save hours to build for a two-week vacation, or is the policy use-it-or-lose-it if you don't cash in from year to year?*

Most services rely on the temp to keep track of total hours, and then they verify the temp's calculations when the temp comes to claim his or her vacation. For this reason, it is a very good idea to *keep both your paycheck stubs*

Figure 6. Sample instructions for filling out timesheet.

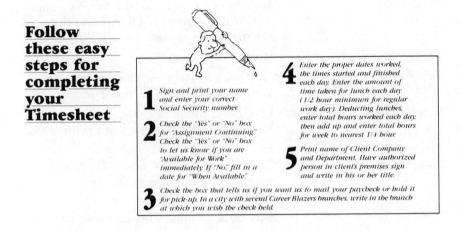

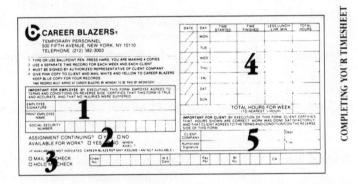

Reprinted by permission. © 1988 Career Blazers. May not be reproduced in whole or in part without the express written permission of Career Blazers.

and a copy of your time sheet for every assignment (or week) that you work.

We spoke with several temp services, large and small, some national firms and some independent owners, to see how temps were faring on the benefits front. Of the twenty services we surveyed, only three did not offer some form of fringe benefits to their employees. Following is a sample of their plans.

Benefit	Condition
Holiday pay	Majority of services want you to work a minimum of 370+ hours in a thirteen-week period *and* the day before and after the holiday.
Vacation (one day)	Must work 416 hours.
Vacation (one week)	Must work 1,300 hrs. within one year. Must work 1,000 hrs., no time frame.
Vacation (two weeks)	1,800 hours within first year, 1,800 hours in second year and a minimum of 1,500 hours the first year.
Longevity bonus	Cash bonus after 2,000 hours of work with no more than six-month gap between assignments.
Merit increase	After three months } Increase base rate After six months
Major Medical	50 percent of premium paid by service, 50 percent by temp. Service pays full premium if temp works thirteen consecutive weeks, minimum 30 hours per week.
Attendance bonus	Cash paid to temps who show up for and complete all accepted assignments in a thirteen-week period.
Child-care reimbursement	(Rare) Allotment given to temps with children under six years of age, primarily in medical market.
Referral bonus	Cash incentive paid to temp who refers another temp and referred temp works specified number of hours for service.
Training	350 hours of employment 100 hours of employment Up to $100 tuition reimbursement on an approved outside course
Employee of the Month	Lunch for two Cash incentive Jewelry
Gift program	Temps earn points for every hour worked, save points toward gifts in catalog (luggage, TV, and so forth).

Helene Kenyon of Debbie Temps in Niles, Illinois, reports:

Our newest benefit is a credit union. Employees can get a loan at a lower rate than at a bank, or a payroll savings plan at a higher rate. . . . Temps need to deposit twenty-five dollars to join; there is no required number of hours for this benefit.

The overall benefits and their conditions are as varied as the temp services themselves. You will need to shop around to see what the services in your area offer.

Temporary services are currently worried by recently proposed health-care legislation. The Minimum Essential Health-Care Act proposed by Senator Edward Kennedy requires all employers, including temporary help firms, to provide a minimum package of health insurance benefits to all full-time employees, who are defined as people who work more than 17.5 hours per week, with no preexisting conditions attached. Under the proposed Act, employers would pick up 80 percent of premium costs, employees, 20 percent. This worries temp services, which argue that they would be forced to insure a large number of people who sometimes work for them for only a very short period of time. At the time of this writing, the legislation is still pending.

YOUR RIGHTS AS A TEMP

As a temp, you are an employee of the temporary help firm for which you work. Like all employees, civil rights laws of both the state and federal governments exist to protect you. Some points of law of which you should be aware follow (note that these apply to all employees, not just temps).

- A temporary service may not discriminate based on race, color, sex, age, religion, or national origin. You can be asked to take a test designed to qualify you for a particular position, but a service cannot screen out a disproportionate number of members of a particular class.
- The Equal Pay Act of 1963 prohibits wage discrimination based on sex for equal work in jobs that require substantially equal skill, effort, and responsibility, and are performed under similar work conditions.
- The Age Discrimination in Employment Act of 1967 prohibits discrimination in employment against individuals between the ages of 40 and 70.

If you feel you are being treated unfairly, bring it to your employer's attention. If the matter cannot be resolved, you should proceed in the most appropriate manner. If you have questions about Equal Opportunity policy, you can address your concerns to:

The EEO Commission
National Office
2401 E Street N.W.
Washington, DC 20507

Temporary services are also subject to federal and state laws governing wages and hours. Temporary services must pay at least the current minimum wage under the Fair Labor Standards Act. A temporary is entitled to overtime pay for any hours worked in excess of 40 hours in one week. It does not matter whether you were at several assignments during the course of the week . . . your total hours worked for the temp service determine you overtime pay. Questions about pay may be addressed to your State Fair Employment Practices Agency or your State Commission For Human Rights. Another resource is:

The U.S. Department of Labor
200 Constitution Avenue N.W.
Washington, DC 20210
(202) 523-9475

THE NATIONAL ASSOCIATION OF TEMPORARY SERVICES

The National Association of Temporary Services (NATS) is the only national trade association for temporary employment services. Founded in 1967, it provides legal, legislative, regulatory, and industry-specific activities/information on behalf of its temporary help service members. Currently, over 600 temporary help services are members. These services operate more than 5,600 offices in the United States, and represent approximately 80 percent of the total industry sales of temporary help services.

We suggest you consider temping with a service that is a member of NATS. Member services must adhere to a code of ethics, which gives you some protection as a temporary employee. While there are very good services that may not be NATS members, we believe membership implies an interest in the industry and a concern to see that the temporary help industry grows under knowledgeable leadership.

NATS produces some excellent literture for both individuals interested in temping and organizations seeking to utilize temporary help. In order to find out more about their publications and the temp industry in general, you may contact them at:

National Association of Temporary Services
119 South Saint Asaph Street
Alexandria, VA 22314
(703) 549-6287

Chapter 5

MY LIFE AS A TEMP

What do temps think of temping?

As with all jobs, some love it, some hate it. For some it's a stepping-stone to something else; for others, a sort of fueling stop; still others see it as a way of life.

Almost anyone who has ever temped for three months or longer can offer you one or two personal experiences that border on the bizarre. Paul Minx, a Manhattan playwright, has temped on and off for eight years and has mastered more than nine PC software packages, as well as the Wang word processing system. Usually, Minx commands *beyond* top wages; because of his superior skills and genial personality, he never lacks for an assignment when he wants one. Here are three of his real-life temp experiences, provided for your amusement. Expect the unusual!

DIARY OF A TEMP
by Paul Minx

To Temp Or Not To Temp

I was sent out to be a Wang temporary at a well-known wine and champagne importer. I was replacing a woman—let's call her Myra—whose desk sat prominently in the center of the Wang area. Myra was the terror of the office, a large woman who though not the office manager, acted like one. She frequently monitored personal phone calls and went through everyone's desk after hours. I was told that the office staff always looked forward to her vacations, taken the second week of June every year. I must admit, they seemed very happy to see me.

The only problem was that Myra never actually went anywhere. She sat at home, caught up on her soap operas, and called the office every couple of hours. I felt like my primary job at this company was deflecting Myra's calls. I spoke with her over fifteen times in a five-day period. She repeatedly reminded me that I was to touch nothing on or in her desk. I was warned never to open one of her desk drawers; and if I wanted something (even a pen or stationery), I should get it from someone sitting near me. Naturally, this aroused my curiosity. The second day, after an extensive debate with myself, I opted to see what personal treasures Myra was afraid the world would seize if given the opportunity. One entire drawer was filled with wrinkled Kleenex tissues, notes to herself (e.g., "buy Kitty Litter"), and duck sauce handouts from a local Chinese restaurant. The drawer below it contained religious paraphernalia, such as religious pictures, several copies of the New Testament, and old church programs.

I don't know what I expected, but it wasn't that. Some desks are best left alone.

Temp Mama

There is a department at a large insurance company that is famous among New York City temps. In this office resides the "Temp Mama," a woman widely known for the hospitality and good cheer she showers on temps. The service asks those of us who go there to take a cut in pay because working conditions are so out of the ordinary.

When I arrived at my workstation, I found a small bouquet of flowers, with a note attached to it: "Welcome to your desk." Beside it was a chocolate croissant and an empty coffee cup with a Post-it note stuck inside, which read: "Fill Me Up." Soon I was greeted by Temp Mama herself. This middle-aged woman with prematurely grey hair could have substituted for any Miss America in the smiles department. She asked me if I was happy, if everything was to my satisfaction—and I could truthfully answer yes, even though I had only been there ten minutes. I assumed she was going to review what I was to do that day, but instead she took me on a guided tour of the office. She introduced me to everyone from the mail clerk to the vice-president. Temp Mama showed me the men's room, even going so far as to take me inside, knocking on a stall door, and inviting me to inspect the facilities. After continuing on to the copier room, the employees' lunchroom, and the supply closet, she took me back to my desk. I still had no idea of what I was to do and was even more curious as to what Temp Mama's daily job entailed. The rest of the day I sat at my desk, answered a few phone calls, and tried to look busy. I later

*learned that this company is famous for assignments like this, and that
most temps said they sat at their desks counting the visits from Temp
Mama!*

Beware the Practical Joker

*There is a brokerage house in the Wall Street area that seems to be the
setting for more than a typical number of eccentric temp experiences.
When I was there I met Mr. Myers, a balding vice-president who made
my life hell. Mr. Myers enjoyed playing practical jokes, especially on un-
suspecting temps. Occasionally (not often), you will run into the permanent employee who thinks you are there to give the natives a few laughs.
The day I was there, Mr. Myers asked me to deliver a very important
envelope to a Mrs. Mercedes Taylor. He told me that she was on the twentieth floor and that "you'd better get hopping. She has a mean temper."*

*We were on the nineteenth floor. Myers had told me that the fastest
way would be to take the stairs. I dutifully went into the stairwell, and
the door slammed shut behind me. I climbed up to the twentieth floor
only to find a sign that read "No Access on This Floor" staring back at
me. I banged and banged, but no one came. I went up to twenty-one,
twenty-two, and twenty-three, but I kept finding the same sign. I knew
this building had over fifty floors, so I started downward. When back on
nineteen I started banging again, but didn't get any response. I thought
that I could hear someone laughing on the other side, though by this time
I could have been hallucinating. I started down the stairs and didn't
bother stopping until I reached ground level.*

*I tore open the important envelope, saw that it contained blank paper,
and threw it in a trash receptacle. I was traveling light that day and had
everything I needed in my suit jacket, so I called my service and headed
for the subway. I decided this was one temp assignment I didn't need.*

TEMP PROFILES

On a more serious side, following are views on life as a temporary employee
from a broad range of temps in a variety of fields.

Ghenia Websterss, Brooklyn Heights, New York

Ghenia Websterss has been temping for approximately seven months. After
leaving a permanent position as an administrative assistant to a senior-level
executive, Websterss decided she would give her "brain a break" and temp
until she decided which direction she wanted her career to take.

Websterss, who changed the spelling of her name based on her belief in numerology, says, "It's what's in my paycheck that counts, not the everyday responsibility." Websterss registered with several services and found one she is very satisfied with. She does warn newcomers, though, that you have to call services and remind them you exist, or else they may stick with their own pool of familiar temps.

> *I don't treat temping as though it were any less important than a permanent job; I'm there to work. It is surprising how many companies are unprepared for you, even though they placed the order for a temp. You can wait awhile before they have any real work for you. . . . I find that there is a tendency to give temps the idiot jobs. But, like I said, it is the paycheck, not the responsibility, that matters most to me. I can't be bothered getting offended by what I'm asked to do. I convey this attitude, and people are usually responsive and relieved. I even volunteer for jobs—the other day I went to the bank for the client.*
>
> *When you go to an assignment, you either sit at a person's desk who is out or you find an empty desk that is generally designated as the "temp desk." Right now, I have been at the same assignment for several months. They are not making full use of my secretarial skills, but my service is still paying me fifteen dollars an hour.*

Webstersss' assignments have included investment houses, corporate legal departments, and an architectural firm. We asked if she had considered any of her temp jobs as a permanent position. "If I saw something I liked, I would pursue it. People have asked for my résumé, but I haven't seen anything of great interest so far. But I'm still looking."

Does she like temping? "Yes. It suits me just fine for now." Webstersss is a tarot card enthusiast, and says she was advised by several psychics not to take a permanent job this year.

> *I've had a good opportunity to get rested and work when I want and where I want. I called in sick one day while on this long-term assignment, and the client refused my service's offer to send another temp in my place. They said they'd wait for me until I felt better. It was nice to see that they appreciated the quality of my work. Temping has been a good option for me. I like the exposure to companies, and I'm very relaxed now.*

Leslie Fallon, Huntington Beach, California

Leslie Fallon is a registered pharmacist.

> *I quit a management job at two pharmacies, which I had held for a total of four years. I didn't know what I wanted to do, so I took two months off and then I decided to try temping. I found I really enjoyed it because*

I wasn't locked into a particular place. . . . I like it for the freedom, convenience, and versatility. Also, it is a great challenge to walk into a new environment and handle a new set of problems each time I temp. There are always new people to meet. . . . I don't find myself falling into a rut.

Some people thought I should pursue regular employment, but temping is my choice. I really like learning new systems, going to new areas, [and] the exposure to different doctors and their therapeutic regime. I also got married and was able to take one-and-a-half months off and come back with no problem.

I repeatedly go back to the same pharmacies. It is kind of like going back and seeing old friends. You increase your scope of colleagues and acquaintances. I learn new uses of medicine from new doctors. I can get a wider view of patient problems and what doctors prescribe as opposed to one small group of the same people where the opportunities and the doctor-patient relationships are more limited. If I should look for a full-time position, I can now eliminate what I'm not comfortable with, and temping lets me know what is available in the market. . . . The flexibility gives me personal time. I've worked long enough now to want more than two weeks off a year.

The pay scale may or may not be a disadvantage. I often have long-distance drives. You work without benefits or insurance, but that is not a problem for me because I have coverage through my husband. Sometimes I find myself overscheduled. I end up working more days than I want to; but if I let my service know there is a problem, they handle it for me.

Newcomers to the field should be flexible and come in with a good attitude. Make an effort to blend with people. . . . Step into a job as if you were working there full-time and not just temporarily. Your attitude makes you act more responsibly, and your peers on the job will appreciate it. . . . Make sure you don't try to make permanent changes in their procedures.

James Kennedy, Dallas, Texas

I started out temping by using a number of different firms. . . . I wanted a lot of different experiences and variety. I used it to shop for a permanent position, a place I could call home. But after temping for over three years, I find I really like being a consultant and I intend to temp forever. For me, consulting work provides (1) a monetary advantage, (2) respect as an expert, (3) a variety of work, and (4) freedom from office politics. The only disadvantages are covering my own health benefits, and there are no other traditional company perks—you have to handle all of this yourself.

Evaluate yourself carefully. You need very strong skills in an area of concentration. Usually you are brought in for "hot" situations, a huge project, or for your special expertise and/or ability to train other employees. You'll need good communication skills and a calm personality to handle any stress you may pick up from those around you. . . . If your area of expertise dries up, it is an economic problem, and you may be out on the street; so keep aware of what is happening within your field. I believe the very best consultants are never without work. A firm will even invent work to hold on to someone whose skills they value or have a need for somewhere down the line.

Anna Marie DeLeyer, St. James, New York

Anna Marie DeLeyer is a career temp. She earns her living through temping. Five days a week and on occasional Saturdays, DeLeyer spends her day caring for elderly shut-ins. She has been at one assignment for over three years. From 9 A.M. to 1 P.M., Monday through Friday, DeLeyer goes to the home of a 96-year-old woman and helps her daughter care for the woman. "It gives the patient's family an opportunity for some personal time," says DeLeyer.

DeLeyer is a personal care nurse's aide, and she enjoys her work. "I get real satisfaction. . . . People appreciate what you do for them." DeLeyer's case load has included many elderly people (70 years and more) with various problems, ranging from retardation to recovery after a hospital stay, as well as taking care of a young girl with cerebral palsy. "This type of work can be emotionally draining, especially if the person is a screamer or complains a lot." DeLeyer, now 25, is an even-tempered, happy person whose first love is horses. Five years ago, DeLeyer, who went to college for two years and studied art and nursing, discovered temping by accident. She joined a service, and along with a group of women primarily in their early twenties through late thirties, took an eight-week, six-hour-a-day training course offered by the service. "We were taught by a registered nurse. Course work covered various medical conditions and terms, patient care, an overview of household chores, and the operation of equipment such as hospital beds and wheelchairs." DeLeyer continues to take in-service training from her service, which is offered to temps at no charge; in fact, they are paid for attending sessions. A nurse from the service visits DeLeyer at her assignment on a monthly basis to check her performance and to issue periodic take-home tests. Some days DeLeyer also works afternoon assignments, and will take on a Saturday assignment, on occasion, if her service needs her. Most temps in this field work on long-term assignments and receive from $5.00 to $6.50 an hour, depending on the assignment and the temp's education and training.

A typical day for DeLeyer includes getting her patient up, bathed, dressed, and fed. She also performs such chores as shopping for groceries, vacuuming, and doing the dishes. "If you are comfortable with the patient and they are comfortable with you, they ask to keep you there." To prove the seriousness of this statement, the granddaughter of De-Leyer's 96-year-old patient told us, "Anna Marie is like family now. . . . We would be lost without her."

Susan Press, New York, New York

Susan Press is a singer and an actress. She graduated from college in 1984 and temped until 1986, when she left temping to go on a national tour. "A lot of actresses do waitressing, which I didn't do well. I turned to temp work as a receptionist, which was great."

Press spoke highly of her service and praised the counselors she worked with.

They opened doors for me and told me they can always get me work. They tried to place me on assignments that were convenient to where I lived and at places from which my performing career could benefit, such as advertising agencies, so I could always leave my photograph and ré-sumé behind. I also always requested one-, two-, and three-day assign-ments because a long-term commitment can be a problem for an actress— I want to be free to go on auditions whenever I need to.

I feel that my temp counselor always worked hard for me. If you are considering temporary work, you must understand the obligations you have to your service. You must keep your commitments when you agree to work. Give 100 percent to your job . . . you have to give in order to get. If you give to the counselor by honoring your commitments, you will always get called to work.

Ron Denecour, Mission Viejo, California

Ron Denecour is a chemist.

I turned to temp work after being laid off from my job. I had thought about going into consulting work before and felt this was the right time. I have been temping now for six months, and see myself doing it full-time. I'm 59 years old, and that makes it hard for me to find a permanent job; but the temporary route has worked very well. I work as a consultant and take care of my own benefits. My service finds the client and takes 25 percent of the fee; I get the rest.

My service manages the bills, and I don't have to hassle to get my money. . . . It's really worth it to me to have no problems collecting money from clients. . . . Temping is good for the older worker—you can be sure of a paycheck without the fear of a layoff. I wanted to go into chemical manufacturing, and temping has been a good solution. I have money coming in, and I'm working in my profession; it looks good on your résumé to be working in your own field while you are in between jobs. If there wasn't subtle discrimination against the older worker, I'd probably look for something permanent; but I feel vulnerable because of my age.

The disadvantages? Well, you work only when clients need your services, which is not necessarily when you need to work. There is some financial insecurity; you need to budget because you don't know what you'll be doing from one month to the next. I have my own lab, too, and this is expensive to keep up. It can be risky, so I take whatever assignments I can get.

My advice to others depends on the individual's objective in temping. I don't think it makes sense to do temp work full-time unless you are a free spirit, or have a special need. I temp to bypass age discrimination. It's not a bad idea to use it to find a permanent job, or if you want to change your career path and want to investigate new possibilities. You must remember, the responsibility for your career is your own.

Judie Collard, Greenfield, Wisconsin

Judie Collard, married and the mother of six children, temps so she can have maximum control over her career.

I've been temping for three years; I like a lot of variety. I can control the time when I don't want to work, so I have time to travel with my husband, have outings with friends, and take care of my household. It allows me time for a social life and time for my children. . . . Temping is great for the working mother. . . . I enjoy temp work for its flexibility, but I do think you sacrifice salary and benefits to get this control.

I learn a lot on every new assignment. Right now, I'm working at an ad agency. I prefer people-oriented assignments. Every time I learn a new way to do something, I bring this shortcut with me and I can pass my skills on to others. . . . You learn on the job, but it is basically through your own initiative or by watching. There is rarely someone there to train you. . . . I get "stressed out" occasionally because when you temp, it is like starting a new job over and over again. Fortunately, the stress level is lower because you know an assignment will end. If I do get too tense, I just tell my service that I'm not available until x date, so I can control it.

My family moved from Wisconsin to Arizona and then back again. I was with a national service, so my work history could carry from one state to another. My hours, records, test scores, and recommendations came with me, and it made it easier for me to find temporary employment.

I tell new temps not to be rigid, to be flexible, and to be able to do a good job without the benefit of being able to see a project through to the end. It is a good experience if you want to control your time or earn extra money. You do need to have confidence in yourself, so you are not intimidated by new people at new assignments. . . . If you don't understand something, ask! One thing I do (and I think others should try it) when I'm on a new assignment—on the second day, after I've settled in—I bring in a glass jar filled with candy and put it out on my desk. Everyone stops to have some candy and talk to me, so it is a really good icebreaker. People remember me for it and are apt to be more friendly and helpful.

Debbie Schlender-Way, Sunnyvale, California

Debbie Schlender-Way temped for over a year as a word processing operator and was ultimately hired in a permanent capacity by one of the companies where she had been on a two-month assignment.

I can operate a lot of different systems: an IBM PC, a Displaywriter, an NBI, a Lanier, a Macintosh. It was easy to pick up different equipment after a while; you can teach yourself.

I first got involved in temp work because I was very unhappy in my permanent job. So, I quit and signed up with different services. I was working within two days. . . . It's a good way to find full-time work. I had three or four job offers within a year at my assignments. When I got married and moved to California, I continued to temp. I was able to find out exactly what a job was all about before committing to it full-time; eventually, I went permanent at an assignment.

It can be frustrating waiting for a client to trust you. First, they watch to see what you can do; sometimes you get bored waiting for them to come around. You also miss the benefits when you temp for some services. . . . My advice would be to sign up with as many services as you can. Be particular about the jobs you take. Don't necessarily take the first job that comes your way. You can always tell a service you'll get right back to them and then check with another service to see if they have a more interesting assignment for you. . . . There is a lot of work out there; so you can afford to select jobs that appeal to you.

Deborah Trotter, San Francisco, California

Deborah Trotter is an attorney currently temping in California.

I worked for a large-size law firm in San Francisco for a few years, but I really didn't enjoy it. I went to a smaller firm where I met people who were doing temp work. When I left that position, I looked for temp work

for myself. I don't see myself working full-time right now. . . . I'm temp-
ing primarily because of my child, and I like the idea of taking time off
when I need to. My husband works at a big San Francisco law firm, and
I have occasionally used his office library on weekends. Even if I didn't
have a child, I think I would work on a temporary basis because I like
the freedom and flexibility it offers.

One of the main advantages is the lack of stress. You are not on the
fast, or partnership, track. You can pick and choose your assignments.
The money is good; I get paid hourly. If I work eighty hours a week, I get
paid for all of them; but if an associate at a law firm works eighty hours,
he or she just gets straight salary. I also like seeing the inside of a variety
of firms; it is a real learning experience, although it is sometimes difficult
to get used to the varying routines.

The last place I worked as a temp before my son was born was a major
law firm, and they treated me just like one of their associates. I haven't
experienced it; but for some, there may be a concern about status and
respect from your peers if you work on a temp basis. However, since
associates move around a great deal, I don't think this is much of an issue.

Albert Rego, Mission Viejo, California

Albert Rego is a scientist.

I worked as a temp to optimize cash flow while I was trying to get my
own business off the ground. As a technical person, you can go in and
address a problem from a scientific viewpoint, without worrying about
the bureaucracies of the organization. You are also able to work more
efficiently; you have the power to make decisions because you have been
hired as a technical expert. . . . You also find a certain prestige associated
with your position. People do what you ask without question. When you
are technically competent, people respect your intellectual expertise.

I advise a new temp to negotiate up-front. Once you are on the job,
there is no leverage as to salary, job specifications, and so forth. Also—
for tax purposes—go in with your last name as a corporation. Present
yourself as a company, not as an individual. . . . Make it clear to the
client that you are not dependent on them; they are dependent on you for
your expertise. And make sure you understand the parameters of the job,
because it is your reputation that is on the line. You have to be competent
to be called back. If you are going to make a career out of temping, make
sure your service understands your goals up-front; and whether you want
to continue to work as a temp or parlay your temp job into full-time
employment . . . they need to know what you're about or else they can't
help you.

Casey Bosco, New York, New York

Casey Bosco knows five software packages: MultiMate, WordPerfect, WordStar, Microsoft Word, and Symphony. She earns approximately $17 to $22 an hour as an evening temp.

I have the job a lot of temps want, and those of us who have them don't want to give them up. Mostly, I work the five P.M. to midnight shift or midnight to seven A.M. I love night assignments, but it took me a while to find them. You just can't walk into a service and expect to get them. In this city, there is a whole family of nighttime temps who know each other from seeing the same faces at different companies. You tell each other which services have the best assignments; a whole network develops. . . .

It's hard to break into it. We got in on the ground floor of word processing around seven years ago. I also know several dedicated word processing machines like Wang and Syntrex. Most of my assignments are law firms, or places where there is a large volume of text that needs to be keyed in before the next workday.

The best part? The money is great; sometimes I get supper and cab fare home. It's not good if you want to meet new people or find a permanent job. There is a limited number of personnel on at night. What I do love is having beautiful days for myself. Usually, I sleep in the afternoons.

Build your proficiency on several systems and temp days first. Make your service love you, and let them know you are very open for evening work. Don't get discouraged; the night work is out there, but you may have to look for it—not every service gets evening job orders.

April Dillon, East Elmhurst, New York

April Dillon now works as a full-time temp counselor for the temp service that once sent her out.

I started temping because I was looking for a permanent job. . . . It let me pay my bills, go on interviews, and minimize stress while job hunting. I temped for approximately two months. . . . What I liked best about it was that it gave me a chance to see what a company was like in terms of atmosphere and people, who had the window offices and why. I learned about the firm's personnel policies and whether there were any good opportunities at the firm.

As a temp, your salary does fluctuate; but if you get good references, you'll always get work. You can be away from your temp service for long periods; but if you had a good reputation with your counselor, they will always be glad to see you again and find work for you. . . . If you want to work in a corporation, go in dressed the part on your very first interview with the service.

Once I was in a large office as an executive secretary and there were four conference rooms. A client came in and only knew a name of someone at the meeting he was to attend. I didn't have any information about the person or the meeting, so I told the client I would need to check with my supervisor. He started to demand the number of the conference room and ran around ranting and raving, opening doors. . . . I tell temps to stay calm and keep your head because not everyone you work with will keep theirs.

Jerry McLoughlin, Bergenfield, New Jersey

Jerry McLoughlin is a certified public accountant who is 65 years old and finds temporary work to be a good way to extend his career.

When I passed retirement age, I was let go. . . . I experienced some difficulty in finding another permanent position, so I sort of backed into temping several years ago. It has kept me busy ever since; work can fluctuate from a one-day job to a year-long assignment.

To get the money—or more than I'm getting at my service—I couldn't get that on an annual basis in a permanent job. . . . If I want to go to the doctor or take six weeks off and go on vacation, I can. It is like I'm an independent contractor. Another advantage is that I'm on a retirement plan with my service—profit sharing. If you put in x number of hours each year, you become part of this plan. You are allocated a certain percentage of the service's profits. It has worked well for me. I'm fully funded now. It has built up a nest egg for me.

Some temps complain about the lack of benefits. And you are always on the road at different clients, that's not a plus or minus for me. . . . It's not very different because when you do public or private auditing, you are always at different offices. I have heard that if you temp for too long (over six months), some offices are not impressed. Temping seems to have a stigma in certain circles. People may think you can't hold down a steady job.

Doing temp work is a good way to work into a permanent spot; but if you are over fifty-five years old, it may be rough to find something permanent. Temping is a good permanent option. Get with a firm that can keep you busy. Register with other services if you are not getting enough work. It can be very discouraging to sit home and wait for a call. . . . Call them when you want to work—let them know you want to work.

Lorraine Beaulieu, New York, New York

During the tourist season, from April through October, Lorraine Beaulieu is a motor coach tour guide. Then she vacations until after the Christmas holidays and temps from January until April. It is a career life-style in which she makes all of her own rules.

I started temping as a receptionist at a bank. While I was there, I learned a word processing system, QYX, and worked for the bank for another month, which gave me some time to practice. Learning QYX doubled my income from five dollars an hour to ten dollars per hour. The next thing I did was go to school to learn Wang word processing; and now I work for a minimum of fifteen-fifty an hour, sometimes as much as eighteen dollars an hour.

I advise people to learn word processing. . . . Anyone can learn it. . . . Learn everything you can about it. If you can run the machine, you can do the work. Lots of secretaries envy me because of the freedom I have, and I make more than they do. I work as much or as little as I want. I don't have to deal with office politics; and if I don't like an office, I can ask to leave. . . . A lot of people wish they could do that.

Tina Clarke, Seattle, Washington

Tina Clarke is a writer who temps to "keep herself in typing paper." She says, "I couldn't be a writer and not have some sort of backup to pay the rent." Clarke temps as a typist or secretary and gives herself creative breaks whenever she needs them and can afford them.

There are two things people never tell you about temping, and I'm not embarrassed to say them. One, I'm a bit of a snoop; and if you temp, you are a legitimate voyeur. You sit at people's desks and you look at their photos, their knickknacks, and their bulletin boards. . . . You find out all about them without ever meeting them. People don't know how much they give away about themselves by what they do with their desks. I use an individual's idiosyncrasies in my stories; as a writer, I find it is a great way to build character development. Second—and this is a nice plus— temping can be a great way to meet men. You can build a social life for yourself. Of course, not just dates. I've made alot of female friends from temping, too. But . . . it is definitely a good way to get introduced to someone in a safe setting. If you see a man in his work environment, you get to know more about him right away. . . . I don't mean to be flip; but apart from the obvious reasons everyone gives for temping, these two stand out for me.

Jerry Pitts, Phoenix, Arizona

Jerry Pitts turned to temping twelve years ago when he was in the process of changing jobs. "I was recently divorced; I was trying new things. . . . Temping let me organize my life without the hassles of really thinking about work." For one of his assignments, Pitts was sent to an office and was told he would handle sales and customer information for a new dog-walking service. "They put me in this large empty room with just a desk and a telephone. . . . I thought it was a little weird. Then the phone started to ring, and while I was on the phone, people came in and dropped off their dogs. Soon I was surrounded by five barking dogs. . . . It seemed like a setup, so I said, 'Is this *Candid Camera?*' and it was!" Pitts was just one of the many individuals surprised by the TV show that used to make good use of temps.

Didn't you always wonder where they got those people to play jokes on? Now you know.

THE BEST AND WORST TEMP ASSIGNMENTS

Now that you've read comments from real temps in the field, let us offer further insight into the kinds of assignments you may encounter from time to time. Here's what we heard from those temps and temporary help services who prefer to keep their anonymity.

The Best

- Serving as a photographer's gofer on photo shoots for a prestigious fashion magazine. The client paid for a three-day on-site shoot in St. Kitt's. "I did everything from ordering coffee to helping the models in and out of their outfits. My travel, accommodations, and food were all taken care of."
- Doing errands for a millionaire investor. "I was given a list of places to go, like the dry cleaner's, cheese shop, and traffic court to pay a parking summons. The best part was I went to each place in the client's chauffeur-driven limousine."
- Shoe modeling. "I wear a size six shoe, and I modeled shoes for buyers at a shoe convention. I didn't get to sit down, but I did get to keep the four pairs of shoes I modeled."
- "We were asked to select a temp to be a fake guest at a theme party where a 'pretend' murder was committed. The guests had to figure out who the murderer was. And you know what? The temp did it!"
- "One unusual assignment I had was serving as a member of a mock jury for pretrial preparations."

- "I assisted the authors in doing the research for this book."
- "It is always easy to get temps to go to the test kitchens at a widely read women's magazine and to have them assist in the preparation and tasting of new recipes."

The Worst

- Washing and stacking clipboards . . . over five hundred of them!
- "Once I and another temp had to hand-address the Christmas card envelopes for a company whose list had 3,144 names."
- Inventory work in a roach-infested stockroom.
- Folding paper bags.
- "Distributing flyers on a city street corner. I was afraid I'd be arrested for littering . . . everyone was throwing them on the ground."

And this story from one temp:

On one of my assignments I was asked to use a transcription machine to transcribe an important interview for a magazine article. There were several of us working to get this project done, and we worked until almost four in the morning because of the crazy deadline. My supervisor stressed that I had to get every word and that the text should read accurately. This wasn't so easy, since the interview took place in a restaurant over dinner and I had to deal with background noise, like conversation from other tables and silverware and dishes clanging.

I listened to one segment for almost an hour. I was in tears because I couldn't get it and the supervisor was making me a nervous wreck. I slowed it down, I sped it up; but still I couldn't get it. After I transcribed the whole tape, I came back to that portion and tried again for about another hour. At 3:30 A.M. we got a call from the person who did the interview, asking how it was going. I told him the section of the tape that was giving me trouble, and I read the counter number to him so he could play his own copy of the tape back. I was really feeling good, like this was a team effort and I was part of this magazine staff.

Suddenly, the person on the other end of the phone starts calling me an idiot and tells me to put my supervisor on. The supervisor listens a few minutes and then looks at me like I'm a moron (even though she couldn't figure out what was being said either). She said since I had finished the tape, I could go home . . . not even a thank-you. I asked what the tape said, and she told me the interviewee was asking the waiter for a cup of cappuccino. I remember I was embarrassed at the time, but now I can laugh at it. Still, it was one of my worst experiences as a temp.

Chapter 6

THE TEN BIGGEST PROBLEMS OF TEMPING

Temping is an industry that is currently experiencing a sort of corporate revolution. Business agrees that it makes economic sense to utilize temps in new ways; and more and more companies are structuring their work flow around temporary employees. While business has made some giant steps in its perception of the temp, the same thing cannot, unfortunately, be said for immediate supervisors, coworkers, and temps themselves. Old myths and traditional temp problems persist.

HOW TO DEAL WITH THE TEMP'S WORST PROBLEMS

Here are ten problems common to temporary employment. You will probably run into at least half of them in your first three months as a temp. It is up to you to deal with these problems in a positive and rational way.

Problem 1: The "Just-a-Temp" Attitude

When a temp arrives at an assignment, he or she is often asked to do tasks that employers may hesitate to ask a permanent employee to do. The "just-a-temp" attitude survives despite the most dazzling temp performances. Why? As a temp you are viewed as someone with no attachments to your coworkers or the company; therefore, they may dismiss you as unimportant or someone regular employees don't have to worry about. This attitude isn't everywhere, but it exists at enough assignments to be a legitimate gripe. It also seems to exist in offices more than in industrial, health-care, and technical areas.

Temps have been around for a long time. The old image of the flaky free spirit or the inept, nail-filing temp haunts many offices. It is hard to lay these ghosts to rest, but the more skilled the temporary workforce becomes, the more the mass perception of temps will change. The temps we spoke with have become resigned to this attitude and say they simply stick out the situation. There is a general understanding of the need for them to demonstrate their abilities and show that they are competent, intelligent people. "It used to make me so mad," said one temp on the West Coast. "I would let them get to me, and it showed in my work. Then I realized I was contributing to their perception when my work was off. Now I go in as some sort of super temp. I get offers for permanent employment all the time. When someone says, 'Why are you temping?' I say, 'Why not?' I tell them there are lots of temps out there like me."

We do caution you not to fall into the trap of assuming the just-a-temp attitude yourself. It takes a positive self-image not to let others make you doubt your abilities. Temps have to work harder than permanent employees to prove themselves. If you want to be treated seriously, then you are going to have to take temping seriously, too.

Problem 2: The Lack of Benefits

We've already discussed this issue in greater detail in Chapter 4, but we bring it up again because it is a frequent and valid complaint of temporary employees.

Bruce Peyton, playwright and former temp, noted, "If you are temping to support yourself and are doing it a long time, especially if you are at one assignment for three months or more, you start to feel like a full-time employee and may resent the lack of benefits." Judie Collard—our office temp from Wisconsin in the last chapter—agreed and brought out another important point:

When I'm ready for an assignment, there may not be one for me. I'm listed with three services, and some of them offer benefits based on the cumulative number of hours you work for them. So if I move around from service to service (which some temps needs to do to earn a living), I can never accumulate enough hours to get the benefits they offer.

If medical coverage, vacation, and other perks are important to you, shop carefully for a service. Understand that you may have to make sacrifices to get the benefits. For example, we know of a service that offers a great benefits package to their temps, but their hourly rates are known to be the lowest in the area. Some loyal, long-time temps work out a deal with their service that allows them to pay a monthly premium (or a portion of it) in order to be covered on the health plan offered to the service's own permanent staff members. We were amazed at the number of temps who simply do not have health insurance coverage. Many say it is too costly to pay on an individual basis, and they are willing to take the risk. The best solution is a purely personal one. Only you will know how important health-care and other benefits are to you and your family.

Problem 3: Social Isolation

It is hard to be a temp if you are the type of person who likes to be friends with your coworkers and enjoys socializing with them outside the workplace. Temps often suffer from social isolation because they are not necessarily treated as one of the gang. This may differ for someone on a long-term assignment: but those temps whose assignments are, for the most part, of short duration find this to be a common problem.

Go to work prepared to brown-bag it for a while. Coworkers are more thoughtless than malicious, so don't get hostile because you haven't been asked out to lunch with a permanent employee. Temps are in and out with regularity, and few people will take the time to get to know you as a person. Temps tell us there is a real camaraderie among temps (from the same or different services) while on an assignment. "You sort of seek each other out like people from the same state while on vacation in Europe."

The best solution is to smile and be friendly. Follow Judie Collard's suggestion of keeping a jar of candy on your desk. Lots of temps tell us the way to even the most unfriendly hearts is through the stomach, and so they bring in home-baked cookies or a box of doughnuts and invite others to share in this treat. You might also offer to lighten a coworker's load if you have the spare time. As a temp, you will get nowhere if you don't make the first move. Don't expect others to be your buddy. If you do develop a rapport, follow up your assignment with a note to your supervisor or coworker saying how much you enjoyed yourself and that you would like to be called again if they ever need you (a humorous card is always well received). Be sure to tell your temp service you want to go back to the company, if possible. We know of one temp who is always called whenever anyone in a particular department is out. She says it's like old-home-week when she's there. And because of the frequency of her visits, she has become familiar with their routine, customers, and personnel in other areas.

If you are on an assignment and you are invited out to lunch, we advise you to go. Beside the possibility of enjoying yourself, it will be to your advantage politically. If you go once and hate it, it is okay to say no the next time—you already made the effort; but do be pleasant.

On the positive side, some temps are so loved by their temporary employer that they get a good-bye party when their assignment ends. One temp told us her coworkers gave her flowers and a card. "Sometimes you do find a kindred spirit . . . and there is instant chemistry."

Problem 4: Work Isn't Always Available When You Want It

This is not true at the time of this writing, but it can and does happen in a tough economy. If you are a temp who wants to work every day, tell your temp service. Orders are always coming in. If your service says it has nothing, say that you are flexible about using less-than-maximum skills and receiving a lower pay rate. We are going on the theory that some work is better than no work.

You might also ask your service whether it wants you to be a standby temp. These are individuals who report to the temp service first thing in the morning. They have yet to be given an assignment, and usually they wait in the service's reception area to see if an order which they can be sent out on comes in. Emergency replacement calls are made daily from clients, and there is always the inevitable no-show temp. You can save your service's reputation by going right out in a pinch. Standby temps are usually paid for a minimum number of hours regardless of whether they are sent out or not.

Most temp services say you can never make a pest of yourself by calling in twice a day and saying you are available. Now is the time to build loyalty and credibility with your service if you plan to temp for a long period. In the future, if we experience any kind of recession, there will be many more temps competing for a smaller number of jobs.

Problem 5: Getting Dumped On

Unfortunately, we have heard this complaint on more than one occasion. Permanent employees find it relatively easy to make the temp their own slave. Sometimes the dumping is in the form of too much work (for example, "Let's give it to the temp, ha-ha!"); and at other times, the dumping is done by making the temp a scapegoat. It's common for a trusted permanent employee to put the blame on the temp if the permanent worker makes an error. They'll say things like "The temp did it," or "It wouldn't have happened if the temp hadn't messed me up."

Don't let the permanent staff bully you. If you let it happen, you will be taken advantage of, particularly if you happen to be competent at what you do. Speak up. Usually one person has the ultimate responsibility for the temp (this is typically the person who will sign your time sheet). Ask this person if you should be doing the nine different things everyone else has given you to do. The answer will probably be no!

If you are feeling completely abused by a client company, call your temp service and let them know the story. Usually, they are only too glad to act as the intermediary.

Problem 6: Fighting Boredom

This is the other extreme. Some companies request a temp when there is absolutely no need for one. If this happens, you have two choices: Tell them they are paying too much for your services, or—depending on your mood and your pocketbook—keep quiet and look busy. Temps often go prepared for that scenario. Some bring paperbacks, needlepoint, cards and letters to write, and crossword puzzles to every assignment. Others combat this problem by using the available time to teach themselves how to use whatever office equipment is near them, and still others actively pursue further responsibility from the client. "I always ask for more to do. . . . I love their look of surprise," laughs one temp.

Problem 7: Adaptability Anxiety

Temps learn to deal with controlled stress. Think about it. Each time a temp goes on an assignment it is like beginning a new job. You don't know anyone, you don't know what you will be responsible for, and you may be under pressure to perform like a pro. One temp who seemed to have this problem under control told us his secret: "I don't believe there is any job out there, with the exception of cardiac surgery and nuclear physics, that cannot be mastered within two weeks. People who think they are irreplaceable should know better." This temp says he goes in prepared to make the employer's life easier. "They've called for a temp, and they rarely expect a miracle worker. I do my thing, ask intelligent questions, and everyone is happy."

Don't put unnecessary pressure on yourself. Turn your anxiety into something positive. Remember, this job won't last forever; and if it isn't of mutual benefit, you can call your service and say you are wrong for the company. But do give yourself a chance to succeed and feel like a hero or heroine.

Problem 8: Acceptance of Your Limited Power

This is difficult if you are intelligent, savvy, and a problem solver. Frequently, temps enter into chaotic situations and can see things in an objective light. They recognize where the problems lie and may even have solutions for them. The problem is, no one is willing to listen to them. Temps can only do so much. Few are given any degree of responsibility, and they have limited opportunity to make positive changes in the workplace—whether it be redesigning a filing system or creating a new form. Permanent employees don't want to hear your ideas. You are the outsider, and they may resent you, or feel threatened by your ability to overshadow them.

Should you say nothing? No. Make contributions, but do so tactfully and in a nonthreatening way. We know of one temp who wrote his supervisor a memo on the last day of his assignment. In it, he thanked the supervisor for the opportunity to work there and pointed out several individuals who helped make his stay a positive experience. He concluded with some thoughts about ideas he had, and outlined what they were. His memo noted that he was't trying to be presumptious, just helpful, and that he didn't know if his ideas were even practical, since he had a limited understanding of the client's business. In short, the temp handled the situation in a delicate and professional manner, and he was asked back to help implement his ideas. The rule here is that it is not what you say, but how you say it.

Problem 9: No Career Path

Temping tends to be a series of similar experiences. Of course, you can build your level of skill and increase your earnings, but you can't really carve out a career path for yourself. If you have aspirations toward management or a corner office, you won't find it as a temp. Again, it all comes down to what you want to get out of temping. It is fine and acceptable as a permanent career as long as you understand its limitations.

We have met temps who went on to succeed brilliantly in specialty careers. These were motivated high achievers who used temping to expand their business experience, develop valuable networking contacts, and fine-tune professional skills. Before you temp, examine the reality of the situation for you in relation to your goals: Will it help get you where you want to be in life? Is it a good solution for you?

Problem 10: Temp Work May Not Be Treated as Credible Work Experience

This is an area of discrimination you rarely hear about: People who opt to leave the world of temping to pursue permanent employment say that they find they have to justify their temp experiences if they expect to be treated seriously. Be prepared for these questions in a job interview, and don't sound defensive or hostile when you answer them.

Why were you temping?
Do you have any real work experience?

Here is a good sample answer:

I temped in order to get a better understanding of a variety of commu-nications-oriented industries. I've had some wonderful experiences in publishing, public relations, and advertising that I wouldn't have had if I hadn't chosen to temp. It gave me the opportunity to learn that I'm happiest in an advertising environment. I know that because of the work I did at XYZ company, assisting its advertising director. Should I tell you what my responsibilities were?

What employer can argue with a statement like that? Rehearse and plan your answer ahead of time. Further, list your employment as a temp on your résumé as follows:

1986–1988

Career Blazers Temporary Personnel, New York, NY
Administrative Assistant
 * Have undertaken various assignments in areas such as account ser-vices, media buying, and public relations
 * Exposure to advertising at the following firms: Condé Nast, Charter Publishing, J. Walter Thompson, Grey Advertising, and McGraw-Hill, Inc.
 * Familiarity with insertion orders, billing, media schedules, direct mail, press kits, and press releases

No doubt, these won't be your only problems as a temporary employee. We don't want to scare you—just make you aware of what to expect once you are temping. It's really not so different from any career, but having foreknowledge of what awaits you can only help.

Chapter 7

ALTERNATIVES TO TEMPING

As employment professionals, we advocate temporary employment through a reliable temp service. From our vantage point, it offers an individual the best balance between a career and a private life without the struggles of self-employment. We do realize, however, that temping is not for everyone. Those who reject temp work offer these common complaints, depending on their sector of the industry:

- "The pay is too low; I can make more money on my own or in a permanent job."
- "Employment health insurance and other benefits either don't exist at my service or they are too hard to accrue."
- "The insecurity of not knowing if I'll be working next week is too stressful."
- "I want to be able to build ongoing relationships with coworkers. I like to see familiar faces at work."

If you can identify with these concerns, we offer some alternatives to temp work. We defined most popular choices of individuals (and some employers) who opted not to work with a temporary help service.

INTERNAL POOLS OR FLOATERS

An internal pool consists of a core of permanent employees who are assigned to temporary assignments within the boundaries of a single organization. For example, a law firm may employ ten secretaries as floaters. They are sent to various departments within the firm on an as-needed basis. Usually, this activity is coordinated by a unit manager. Floaters generally receive the same pay and fringe benefits as all other workers employed by the organization. They may work full- or part-time, and may even "flex" the hours they work, depending on their employer's project schedule or seasonal need. Floaters do *not* work through a temporary help firm.

A great deal of planning, recruiting, and coordinating is involved in the creation and setting up of a workable internal pool. These pools are most commonly found in large firms (five hundred-plus employees), and their size is always smaller than the organization's peak demand for temporary staff. This is to ensure cost-effectiveness; a firm wants to be sure the floaters it employs are used every hour they spend at the workplace. Even if a firm uses floaters, it will typically supplement its internal pools with the use of outside temporary help as needed. Companies generally like the concept of internal pools, although they are hard to administer. A floater's familiarity with the company's procedures and working environment minimizes the learning-curve factor and maintains continuity. Many floaters are cross-trained so that they can handle a variety of needs. Since floaters have no ongoing responsibilities of their own, they can assist others without having their own work suffer.

We found that people who float usually do so for one of two reasons:

1. As an entry-level mechanism to gain access to a more permanent position within the organization
2. As an exit mechanism for those employees who plan to retire or who wish to work less than a forty-hour week

Typical pool/floater groups include mailroom personnel, messengers, secretaries, personal-computer or word processing operators, bank tellers, nurses, and food-service workers. Floater positions are difficult to find without going through an employment agency, but we did manage to locate one advertisement (Figure 7) from a recent newspaper. Not surprisingly, it is from a law firm.

PART-TIME EMPLOYMENT

A part-time employee works less than a forty-hour week but reports to the same position at regularly scheduled times. A part-timer can work one day per month or every day. An informal survey showed that most part-timers work an average of twelve to twenty-five hours per week. Part-timers may qualify for health insurance coverage and other company benefits, including paid time off, but these fringes are usually applied on a prorated basis.

Figure 7. Ad for floaters at a law firm.

Employers generally have a large pool of candidates seeking part-time work, so they can afford to be selective. Good part-time jobs (those offering convenient hours and high pay) are difficult to find because personnel turnover is so low. A happy part-timer recognizes that he or she has a good deal and is reluctant to give it up.

According to The Conference Board, a research group based in New York City, part-time employment options are most commonly found at companies with a fairly young workforce and those which are largely nonunion. If you prefer a steady part-time job over temporary employment, here are some tips for you to follow.

1. Look for part-time employment at smaller companies (fewer than fifty people); in general, they are more receptive to this option.

2. Approach your full-time employer about the possibility of switching your position to a part-time one, perhaps split between yourself and another part-timer.

3. Pursue part-time leads with as much energy and enthusiasm as a full-time campaign. Follow up your personal network contacts and read the classified newspaper ads with a discerning eye.

4. When you go on an interview, don't write "seeking part-time employment" on your application or on your résumé. Wait until you have met the employer and he/she seems to like you and/or be comfortable with you. Ask what kind of part-time opportunities are available with that organization. If you don't take the plunge and ask, you may miss a wonderful job opportunity.

5. If you find an employer who wants to hire you but is skeptical about part-time work, offer to give yourself and the employer a trial period of ninety days to test each other.

Figure 8 shows some typical advertisements for part-time employment. The newspaper listed many ads, but many of them we found to be for unattractive and low-paying telephone solicitation positions.

Figure 8. Several ads for part-time positions.

P/T
MEMBERSHIP COORDINATOR
Nonprofit resolution dispute association seeks highly-motivated, articulate indiv to assist in membership phone telemarketing & develop prospective membership list. Fund-raising exp a plus. Excel oppty for someone returning to the work force. No phone calls. Send resumes to

PART TIME
INSTRUCTORS
Multi-million dollar educational company has immediate positions available for conscientious individuals throughout the New York, New Jersey and Connecticut area. Teaching experience helpful but not a prerequisite. Excellent opportunity to earn money and supplement family income. Must be available 8:30am-2:00pm. Car required. Per Diem rate.

PART TIME
SECRETARIES
Part time Secretaries wanted to join major sports and entertainment company's in-house temporary employee program. Candidates must have advanced verbal communication skills, proficient Wang word processing skills and type 55 WPM. Tailor your part time schedule according to available temporary assignments. Salary to $15/hr.

PART TIME
Is seeking a TELLER/CASHIER to work in its Accounting Department. The qualified individual should have teller or cashier experience and be able to work the following weekly schedule.
.Thursday, 9:45am-11:30am
.Friday, 10am-12:30pm
.Saturday, 10:45am-6pm
Individuals should also be available to work 12 weeks (35 hours weekly as a vacation replacement).
Please call Mon-Fri 10am-5pm

FLEXIBLE WORK SCHEDULES

Flexitime and job sharing are two options that are most often found within the walls of an innovative organization dedicated to maximizing employee productivity through worker-directed programs. Employees fortunate enough to participate in such programs usually have worked one or more years with the organization as full-time permanent employees, and then convert to flexitime or job-sharing status.

According to the Administrative Management Society, the percentage of American companies offering flexible work schedules more than doubled between 1977 and 1986.

Flexitime

In a flexitime arrangement, an individual works during specific core hours and makes up the rest of his/her workday at hours mutually agreed upon with the employer. Our research turned up one flexitimer who works 7:00 A.M. to 5:00 P.M. Monday through Thursday, with Fridays off; and another, this one a working mother, who works 10:00 A.M. to 2:00 P.M. and 4:00 P.M. to 8:00 P.M. This woman is able to get her kids off to school, be home for their return, and leave again when her husband comes home from work.

Job Sharing

In a job-sharing situation, two individuals share everything: salary, hours, and responsibilities. At our organization, we have two women who share one permanent, full-time sales position. One works two full days; the other, the remaining three. We do caution that in order to make this kind of relationship run smoothly, the two parties must be attuned to each other, keep each other informed of their individual activity, and each must share equally in the workload. When one partner carries the burden of responsibility, resentment is likely to grow and sabotage the job-sharing concept for others.

Companies have found that flexible work schedules have both advantages and disadvantages.

Advantages:

- Company morale is boosted, and employees experience increased loyalty, particularly those with specific conflicts between work and home.
- A firm with flexible scheduling has a competitive edge in hiring and keeping employees.
- Employees feel greater control over their home and at-work activities.

Disadvantages:

- Not all employees make use of flexitime; some people make minimal or no available scheduling changes.
- Morale doesn't necessarily rise if the program isn't used.
- A company that makes extra effort to determine whether its employees are really putting in full days (by installing time clocks, for example) may destroy the freedom and morale lift it was trying to create.

EMPLOYEE LEASING

It may be easiest to think of employee leasing as a management tool for the small-business owner. A typical client of an employee leasing firm might be a doctor's office, a small retailer, or a building/home improvement contractor. The major benefits offered to the user include:

- Payroll provisions
- Group health care at low rates based on the total number of employees handled by the employee leasing firm
- Employer freedom from paying liability taxes, worker's compensation, disablilty insurance, and unemployment insurance

The small-business owner who works with an employee leasing firm generally wants to provide the best possible benefits package available to his existing staff in the most cost-efficient manner.

Employee leasing allows a business to transfer a group of its employees to the payroll of a leasing organization. After the transfer, the employees are leased back to their original employer. These employees perform in permanent positions and follow set hours on a daily basis at the original employer's location.

A contract leasing firm hires an organization's existing employees and then leases them back for a fee. The leasing firm pays all the employee benefits, including pension contributions equal to a percentage of the employee's annual earnings. Since contract leasing firms are generally larger than the customer who utilizes their services, leased employees may benefit by receiving a more attractive benefit program than if they had gone through their original employer. The size of the leasing firms allows them to negotiate the lowest possible premium rates for health-care and life insurance plans for their employees.

Employee leasing firms and their users operate under the Tax Equity and Fiscal Responsibility Act (TEFRA) of 1982 amd the Deficit Reduction Act of 1984. These rules were set up to protect leased employees and to ensure that they could receive employee pension programs and other benefits compensation. The federal government considers employee leasing and temporary help services to be similar industries and has given them the same SIC (Standard Industrial Classification) code.

There is very little an individual can do to become a leased employee. This is largely a decision made solely by the employer (owner); however, if you feel you are not receiving adequate health coverage or pension compensation, you might suggest employee leasing as a alternative to your employer.

PAYROLLING

This concept is closely related to employee leasing. In payrolling, a company may recruit, interview, and select individuals to work at their firm but places those individuals on the payroll of an outside service. Organizations that use the payrolling concept usually do so for workers employed on large projects of limited, but long-term, duration, for example, paralegals working on a large document case.

For the person being payrolled, it is simply like working on a long-term temporary assignment. However, the advantage to the business is that payrolling usually involves a charge of 20 to 25 percent above the salary of the payrolled employee, whereas the charge for a straight temp for the same work is likely to be 30 to 60 percent above salary. Many temporary help firms offer payrolling projects at discounted rates as a special feature to their customers.

INDEPENDENT CONTRACTORS

We could title this section "Temping Without a Service." It is directed at those ambitious individuals who have the tenacity and the agressiveness to take their knowledge of the temporary marketplace and turn it into higher earnings for themselves. It can be done very successfully, but don't allow yourself to be blinded by your potential earnings, since there are some disadvantages and you should be aware of them.

An independent contractor, also known as a free-lancer, is a self-employed individual; he or she is *not* on an employer's payroll, and therefore, no outside source makes deductions for Social Security (FICA) or withholding taxes on his/her behalf. An independent contractor provides specific task-related services to an employer in accordance with the terms of his or her contract with the customer. Many temps are lured into independent contractor status because employers may pay an independent contractor a higher rate than they would pay a salaried employee. In addition, an employer may be willing to pay the independent contractor a higher rate than he or she would have received as a temp for the same job. Why? Because an independent contractor eliminates the middleman, in this case the temporary help service, which may be charging the customer a higher rate for the temp to cover the service's overhead.

In addition to a higher income, many people pursue free-lance work in order to establish a special expertise or professional status within an industry. They find a niche and turn it into a successful business. Independent contractors also have the ability to take tax deductions as sole proprietor of a business. A few words of caution: There is considerable opportunity to violate the rules of this concept, and it is your responsibility to make sure you adhere to them.

As an independent contractor:

You must assume all the financial risks and legal liabilities of owning your own business.

You are responsible for paying state and federal withholding tax and FICA contributions.

You must pay self-employment tax for FICA as both an employer *and* the employee.

You will be taxed on your business earnings, even if you do not consider it a salary.

You must estimate your income on a quarterly basis in order to make federal and state income tax deposits. If you underestimate your earnings, you may have to pay a penalty.

You are responsible for your own health coverage and pension plans.

We could go on and on about self-employment guidelines, but we suggest the best person to advise you is an accountant. Don't pursue employment as an independent contractor unless you feel well-versed in current law and setup procedures.

An independent contractor cannot free-lance without a special expertise and a market that will buy this expertise. You must have perceived value to an organization. Before you go out on your own, get a good overview of what you can offer your clients and who the real buyer of your service will be. It is essential that you be able to build your own client base; so you must not be shy about selling your services. Temps who have taken this route tell us that you should network with employers and working peers. One told us, "Temp through as many services as possible so that you are exposed to a wide variety of companies. Build a reputation and contacts."

Kyle O'Hara is a 28-year-old singer/actor living in Manhattan. Here is his advice for temping successfully without a service.

For three years I worked with two of the city's busiest services. I liked temping, but I knew I could make more money on my own. . . . I knew my service was getting a healthy markup for my work. I decided to freelance when clients began telling me they would gladly pay me directly, and I knew there were enough of them to make me think I would be kept busy. . . . I type one hundred eight words per minute, and I'm proficient on Wang, Syntrex, and Vydec [all word processors]. I also know personal computer software—MultiMate, WordPerfect, Lotus [1-2-3], and dBase. I probably can fudge a few other packages, too—if I had to—they are all very similar. . . . I used one of my head shots from my acting portfolio, and I had it printed on a postcard with my skills superimposed on the image. The back of the card was printed with my name, phone number, and the words "Need a temp? Call me direct." I sent them out everywhere. . . . It started to work. . . . That was four years ago, and business is still great. Of course, working independent of a service was more of a novelty then. I also joined a trade association; I never go to the meetings, but I use names in their newsletter when I want to send out new mailings. . . . I drop out now and then to do summer stock and Off-Off-Broadway work; but when I get back to the city, I send out my cards with a big red stamp "He's back!" printed on my forehead on the postcard. . . . I have a base of about ten steady clients: that's all I need really. Most of my work is actually done at two main companies. . . . I get a lot of referrals, but I send the business to other freelancers I know or sometimes to my old service. . . . More advice? Well, keep accurate records, maintain a good mailing list, keep it updated with names, get permission to use personal references, don't be shy about making collections calls— sometimes trying to get paid is a drag—and don't have a wild message on your machine: Even if it's funny, you'll scare off business.

A FINAL WORD

We hope that we have provided insight and answers to your questions about the world of temporary employment. If there are some matters we have neglected to address, we invite you to send your inquiries to us at:

Career Blazers
Attention: W. Lewis/N. Schuman
590 Fifth Avenue, 7th Floor
New York, NY 10036

All requests will be answered and kept completely confidential.

Let us close with this comment from Howard Scott, president of CDI Temporary Services in Philadelphia: "A great temporary employee is simply a great worker. It's a matter of attitude. You need an overwhelming interest in performing a job as best as you can, . . . to be an exceptional temporary employee is to take great pride in yourself, your work, and your service."

GLOSSARY

To improve understanding of the temporary help business and to help distinguish it from fundamentally different businesses, such as the employment agency business and employee leasing, the National Association of Temporary Services has prepared this lexicon of terms.

agency   an employment agency. *See* employment agency.

applicant   an individual seeking temporary employment with a temporary help company. In the employment agency business, *applicant* means a person seeking to be permanently placed.

assign   the act of sending a temporary employee to work on the premises of a customer of the temporary help company. *Assign* is different from *referral*, which describes the employment agency practice of sending an applicant to a prospective employer for an interview. *Refer*, or *referral*, does not apply to the act of assigning temporary employees.

assignment   the period of time during which a temporary employee is working on a customer's premises.

commingling   *See* joint operations.

coordinator   the staff employee of a temporary help company who assigns temporary employees to work on the customer's premises.

counselor   an employment agency employee who refers or places applicants for employment with employers. The term does not apply to a staff employee of a temporary help company. Many state employment agency laws require that counselors be licensed.

customer   the person, organization, or business that uses the services of a temporary help company.

dispatch   this term is generally used to refer to the act of assigning industrial temporary employees to report for work on a customer's premises.

employee leasing   an arrangement whereby a business transfers it employees to the payroll of a "leasing organization," after which the employees are leased back to their original employer where they continue working in the same capacity as before in an ongoing, permanent relationship.

employment agency   a business whose purpose is to bring a job seeker and a prospective employer together for the purpose of effecting a permanent employment relationship.

fee   the amount charged by an employment agency for placing job seekers in permanent positions. The term does not refer to a temporary help company's gross profit or liquidated damages charge. *See* liquidated damages.

general employer   an employer who has the right to hire and fire an employee, is responsible for the employee's wages and benefits, and exercises ultimate supervision, discipline, and control over the employee. Temporary help companies are the general employers of their temporary employees. *See* special employer.

in-house temporary an individual hired directly by a nontemporary help company as a permanent employee to perform various temporary assignments within that company.

independent contractor a person, not an employee, who performs work for another. Unlike employees, independent contractors (1) are not subject to the control and supervision of the person using the services regarding the details of how the work is to be performed, (2) generally have specialized training or education, and (3) supply all necessary tools, supplies, or equipment necessary to perform the work.

job order *see* work order.

job shop a colloquial term generally used to refer to businesses that supply longer term temporary employees on a contract basis in technical or specialized areas such as engineering, drafting, and so forth.

joint operations the operation of both a temporary help company and an employment agency by the same firm. Problems arise when these fundamentally different operations are conducted with the same personnel, forms, and procedures, so that the two businesses are not easily distinguished by job applicants and customers. Such commingling leads to public confusion about the nature of the temporary help business and could subject the industry to employment agency regulation. To avoid customer confusion, NATS has developed guidelines to help NATS members keep the two businesses separate.

liquidated damages liquidated damages are monies paid by temporary help customers under agreements in which the customer agrees not to hire the temporary employee within some specified period of time and to pay damages for breach of that promise in the agreed upon, that is, liquidated, amount.

part-time a work period less than the full workday or full workweek. Part-time employees are not temporary employees because, unlike temporary employees, they work a regular schedule for their employer on an ongoing, indefinite basis. *See* temporary employee.

payrolling a colloquial term in the temporary help industry that describes a situation whereby the customer, rather than the temporary help company, recruits an individual and asks the temporary help company to consider employing the individual and assigning him to the customer on a temporary basis. Once hired by the temporary help company, the payrolled employee's employment relationship with the temporary help company is the same as any other temporary employee.

placement   an employment agency term describing the act of successfully placing a job seeker in a permanent position with an employer.

special employer   a term referring to a customer's legal relationship to the temporary employees assigned to them. The relationship is based on the customer's right to direct and control the specific details of the work to be performed. As special employers, customers have certain legal rights and obligations regarding temporary employees; for example, because worker's compensation insurance (which temporary help companies provide for their employees) is the exclusive relief available to the employees against employers for work-related injuries, a temporary employee generally cannot sue his special employer (the customer) for negligence. Hence, the customer's special employer status insulates it from such liability. On the other hand, as special employers, customers may also have certain obligations to temporary employees, for example, not to discriminate against them in violation of the civil rights laws. *See* general employer.

supplemental staffing   the term is generally used to refer to the practice of supplementing the permanent staff of hospitals and nursing homes with nurses and other health-care personnel employed by temporary help companies.

temp-to-perm   also referred to as "try before you hire." The practice of sending temporary employees on an assignment for the express purpose of ultimately placing them in a permanent position with the customer. This is an employment agency activity that may subject a temporary help company to regulation under state employment agency laws.

"Temp-to-perm" practices include but are not limited to:

Advertising "temp-to-perm" positions to attract workers seeking permanent jobs.

Suggesting or recommending to customers that they use temporary employees on a "temp-to-perm" basis.

Agreeing to customers' requests to send temporary employees on a "temp-to-perm" basis.

Sending temporary employees to customers to be interviewed for the purpose of determining who will be assigned to the customer on a "temp-to-perm" basis.

temporary employee   an employee who does not make a commitment to an employer to work on a regular, ongoing basis but instead is free to accept (or reject) assignments at such times and for such lengths of time as the employee may choose. A temporary employee is obligated only to complete a particular assignment once one is accepted, but has no obligation to accept further assignments. *See* part-time employee.

temporary help company   an organization engaged in the service business of furnishing its own employees (temporaries) to handle customers' temporary staffing needs and special projects.

try before you hire   *See* temp-to-perm.

work order   an order received from a customer for a temporary help company's services. In the employment agency industry, the term *job order* refers to a request from a prospective employer authorizing the employment agency to find an appropriate prospective employee.

DICTIONARY OF TEMPORARY HELP

Adia Personnel Services, a national temporary help firm with over 400 offices spread throughout the United States, has graciously allowed us to include *The Adia Dictionary of Temporary Help*. This dictionary includes job descriptions for a wide variety of temporary positions within the following categories: accounting, banking, clerical, communications, data processing, marketing, secretarial, typing, word processing, light industrial, and factory/warehouse. We hope this guide will allow you to familiarize yourself with which job description best matches your current skills. (Please note: It is virtually impossible to list *all* categories of temporary help; this dictionary offers a representative sampling of the most popular positions in the temporary help industry.)

ACCOUNTING

Figure Clerk Performs routine accounting duties which do not require knowledge of accounting and bookkeeping principles. Among these are posting simple journal vouchers and reconciling bank accounts. Supervision needed.

Calculator/Adding Machine Operator Performs standardized mathematical computations: addition, subtraction, multiplication, simple division, and percentages. Posts results on record sheets or verifies computations made by others. Must be experineced on one or more machines, such as rotary, printing, electronic calculator, ten-key, or full bank.

Payroll Clerk Performs general payroll functions, including pegboard posting. Calculates payroll tax deductions, quarterly returns, W-2 forms; prepares paychecks. Operates calculator or adding machine by touch. May calculate reports, including totals paid out, commissions, and overtime.

Junior Accounting Clerk Performs light clerical duties within an accounting function. May type, match payments to accounts receivable, check items on invoices and purchase orders. May code and post to accounts, and verify accuracy by checking totals. Will prepare bank deposits and perform other routine calculations with specific instructions. May have light or no prior experience and should be supervised.

Senior Accounting Clerk Knowledgeable in accounting procedures and uses judgment in performing clerical duties. Functions may include posting and reconciling bank or cash accounts and reviewing transactions for completeness. May assist accountant in preparation of reports, answer customer inquiries, and investigate complaints about possible errors. Operates calculator or ten-key adding machine by touch. Works under supervision of accounting supervisor or accountant.

Bookkeeper Compiles, posts, and maintains records of financial transactions. Responsible for verifying transactions and entries into account or cash journal. Summarizes details in separate ledgers, transfers data to general ledger, and compiles reports. May also calculate wages, make up payroll, and prepare tax reports.

Machine Bookkeeper Sets up machine to perform financial transactions, such as payables and receivables. Prepares invoices, statements, or bills.

Bookkeeper, Full Charge Keeps complete systematic records without supervision. Prepares and maintains financial records and vouchers; maintains subsidiary ledgers and control accounts. Prepares trial balances, summaries, and analyses.

Accounting Assistant Analyzes accounts and reconciles differences. Assists in preparation of tax returns and financial reports. Assists with monthly and year-end closings.

BANKING

Posting Clerk   Records transactions in journals, ledgers, and forms. Documents entries from one source to another. May compute debits and credits and use bookkeeping machine.

Proofing Clerk   Sorts, records, and proofs transactions using proof machine. Batches items, either manually or by machine. Follows instructions well.

Reconcilement Clerk   Reconciles statements, makes copies, files them, and compiles reports.

Teller   Provides general teller service to bank customers with high degree of accuracy. This includes receiving deposits; payouts on checking and savings accounts; buying and selling cash; balancing cash drawer; and sorting, counting, and wrapping money. May issue traveler's checks, money orders, and bank checks. Can identify counterfeit bills and forgeries. Can operate microfiche equipment to read and verify balances and signatures.

New Accounts Clerk (40 wpm typing)   Compiles, types, and files lists of new accounts. Duplicates records for distribution to various branches. Records data and keeps records accurately.

Stock Transfer Clerk   Accurately records security transfers, payments, and interest charges. Verifies assignment guarantees, revenue stamps, addresses, and dividends against bank statements. May file debits and credit accounts.

Escrow Clerk   Compiles needed information to process mortgage loans, such as review of borrower's loan papers for completeness. May gather credit information, complete bank papers and instruction forms, and make entries by hand on loan papers. May also maintain card file indicating additions and withdrawals from file. Good at detail, accurate, and neat.

Trust Clerk   Compiles information from files. Records and processes cards and records transactions. Makes simple calculations to determine profit, loss income, and unit quantities.

Encoder Operator   Operates encoder machine to transcribe data onto magnetic tape. Reads tapes for work procedures, sets and removes reels, verifies, and makes corrections.

Bursting Machine Operator   Operates bursting machine which separates, trims, and addresses forms. Verifies and packs forms. Labels boxes for mailing and changes bursting machine ribbon.

CLERICAL

General Clerk Performs basic clerical duties which do not require specialized knowledge of systems and procedures. These may include photocopying, addressing and stuffing envelopes, sorting and distributing mail, light stockroom and messenger duties. Supervision recommended.

Senior Clerk Experienced in systems and procedures and has high level of initiative. May research data and chart statistical information, and routinely process information by tabulating, compiling, sorting, coding, filing, or cross-referencing. Qualified to supervise activities of large mail room, including inventory control.

File/Batching Clerk Files or batches material according to standard systems, such as alphabetic, numeric, or subject. Maintains a log of material which is returned or borrowed, and photocopies materials. Previous experience is not required, so should be supervised to work effectively.

Duplicating Clerk Operates several models of photocopy machines and does basic cleaning and repair maintenance. Produces accurately collated materials.

Inventory Clerk Accurately counts, records, prices, and labels inventory. May also operate calculator or adding machine. Works most effectively with supervision.

Mail Clerk Performs simple clerical work and routine duties connected with mail room activities. May operate standard postage meter, sealer, or mailer machines.

Posting Clerk Accurately and neatly posts basic data from one document to another. Familiar with graphs, charts, and standard forms. Can do simple tabulating of information.

Messenger/Supply Clerk Runs errands and delivers mail, including light packages. Unpacks, distributes, and shelves supplies. Keeps simple records. Does not drive client company vehicles, or handle cash or valuables.

Records Clerk Operates rotary or planetary microfilm equipment for filming and printing. Maintains records, which may include labeling, indexing, posting, coding, sorting, filing, and purging.

COMMUNICATIONS

Receptionist   Good public image and phone manner. Greets visitors, determines the nature of their visits, and directs them to their destinations. May keep visitor and phone logs and perform routine light clerical duties.

Receptionist/Typist (45 wpm typing)   Assigned where poise with the public is needed, where traffic and telephone activity are sporadic, and telephone equipment has fewer than fifty incoming lines. Greets and announces visitors and directs them to their destinations. Takes telephone calls and routes them to employees using a standard set or a call director. May also place calls, relay messages, and maintain logs and directories. Light clerical duties may include typing of forms and routine correspondence.

Call Director Operator   Operates a call director with four to twenty lines. Can process several calls at once, take messages, and screen calls. Pleasant phone manner.

Switchboard Operator   Qualified to operate a switchboard with single or multiple position cords or a variety of cordless switchboards. Places long-distance, WATS, or conference calls. May also record and time-stamp call information on toll cards, and perform other telephone-related duties.

Telex/TWX/Telegraph Operator   Experienced in sending and/or receiving messages using telegraphic typewriters.

DATA PROCESSING

Junior Keypunch Operator (8,000 strokes)   Records or verifies alpha/numeric coded data on tabulating cards.

Keypunch Operator (10,000 strokes)   Experienced in selecting type and number of cards to record or verify complex or uncoded data from source material which may not be organized for keypunch. Prepares drum cards and can decipher from illegible sources and assist in preparing new sources. Can perform standard operations as well as follow special instructions.

Key to Tape/Disc Operator (10,000 strokes)   Experienced operator of non-card-producing data preparation machines, including a shared processor, key entry, or key tape machine.

CRT Operator   Operates CRT to post or retrieve information accurately from raw data. Can log on, inquire, and set to transmit data.

Data Control Clerk   Experienced in controlling computer input and output, working with computer forms, and balancing computer reports.

Data Entry Operator (10,000 strokes)   Does alpha and numeric entry from raw data. Some supervision recommended.

Junior Computer Operator   Experienced in language and systems. Does data entry and operates peripheral equipment. Some supervision recommended.

Computer Operator   Operates computers using established procedures and reports any deviations. Determines the nature of errors or equipment failure and makes normal console adjustments. Maintains machine records, performance and production reports.

Programmer   Experienced in programming language. Works independently to analyze and define programs for electronic data processing equipment. Revises and refines programs and documents through established schedule. Can assist in lower-level classifications and evaluate and modify existing programs to accommodate system changes.

MARKETING

Demonstrator Presents detailed descriptions of a product to an audience in a retail setting. Invites participation and questions from audience. Is well-groomed and articulate, and can memorize and follow directions well.

Host/Hostess Greets guests arriving at gatherings such as trade shows, conventions, business openings, or conferences. May verify names on guest list and provide name badges. Gives directions, hands out samples, fliers, or serves refreshments. May wear uniform or costume. Well-groomed, articulate, and personable, and follows directions well.

Survey Inside Telephones people from list prepared by client to obtain answers to questions. Articulate and persistent despite occasional negative responses. Will work flexible hours and keep simple records.

Survey Outside Obtains answers to client-prepared list of questions from selected group of people. Persists despite negative responses, and achieves cooperation. Well-groomed and articulate. Will travel within designated location.

Sales Inside Telephones prospects from prepared list. Employs prepared presentation, which individual can adapt to various prospects to encourage them to buy the product. Articulate, persistent, and able to keep simple records.

Sales Outside Proven sales ability and persistence coupled with the ability to learn thoroughly about a product or service, or to answer questions and objections effectively. Adept at tailoring presentations to individual needs. Well-groomed and able to keep simple records.

Comparison Shopper Maintains strict confidence when visiting competitors to gather information, such as style, quality of service, price, or employee performance. Assumes customer role and can memorize prepared questions and keep simple records. Well-groomed, observant, and trustworthy.

Convention Booth Attendant Learns about client's product or service and answers questions articulately. Assists in handing out literature or samples, completion of order forms, and may serve refreshments. May wear uniform or costume. Personable and well-groomed.

Display Assistant Maintains and replenishes client's merchandise at retail locations on a designated route. Arranges displays, cleans and checks prices of products. Maintains simple records, and follows directions.

SECRETARIAL

Junior Secretary (50 wpm) Working knowledge of general office procedures. Does straight typing of correspondence and reports. Answers telephone and takes messages. Opens and distributes mail, maintains files and records, gathers information, and performs simple calculations.

General Secretary (60 wpm) Performs secretarial and clerical duties for one or more people. Answers and places telephone calls, distributes mail, receives visitors, maintains files, prepares reports, and makes appointments.

Transcription Secretary (60 wpm) Prepares correspondence, reports, and other technical material with a transcribing machine for one or more administrators. Answers and places telephone calls, distributes mail, and schedules appointments.

Shorthand Secretary (60+ wpm typing; 90 wpm shorthand) Takes and transcribes dictation of all office communications, including correspondence and reports, for one or more administrators. Answers telephone and places calls, receives visitors, distributes mail, and schedules appointments.

Executive Secretary (70 wpm typing; 90 wpm shorthand) Performs secretarial duties for executives in top management positions. Skilled at working with people at all levels within an organization. Takes and transcribes dictation, handles correspondence, prepares reports. Screens telephone calls, schedules meetings and conferences, and makes travel arrangements. Very professional appearance.

Legal Secretary (65 wpm typing; 90 wpm shorthand) Performs secretarial duties with high degree of accuracy, including transcription from shorthand or a dictating machine. Knowledgeable in legal terminology and procedures, and may even specialize in an area of law (for example, tax, patent, or corporate).

Specialized Secretary (55 wpm typing; 80 wpm shorthand) Extensive professional secretarial and clerical experience in a specialized field, such as medicine or engineering. Knows terminology, symbols, forms, and procedures of field. May be bilingual or have other specialization.

Specialized Transcription Secretary Prepares correspondence, reports, and other technical material with a transcribing machine for one or more administrators. Extensive professional secretarial and clerical experience in a specialized field such as medicine or engineering. Knows terminology, symbols, forms, and procedures of field. May be bilingual.

TYPING

Clerk Typist (40–50 wpm)   Does light typing that does not require independent judgment, such as envelopes, labels, and form letters. Performs other basic clerical duties. May have minimal office experience.

Intermediate Typist (50–60 wpm)   Formats and types correspondence and reports using correct spelling and punctuation. Experienced in office procedures.

Senior Typist (60+ wpm)   Formats and types a variety of correspondence and forms. May type from drafts with two or more sources, set up forms and standard tabulations. Knowledgeable in spelling, punctuation, spacing, and syllabification. Performs other general clerical duties.

Reproduction Typist (50 wpm)   Can type copy for training manuals and parts manuals on IBM Executive or IBM Composer. Produces master copies on composer using various sizes and type styles, tabulations, and margins. Makes corrections and justifies margins, and can produce equations and artwork for overhead projection.

Forms Typist (50 wpm)   Does detailed heavy typing—such as purchase orders, sales orders, and invoices, which may require up to ten copies per form. Verifies and types numeric extensions for accuracy and performs simple calculations accurately.

Manuscript Typist (55 wpm)   Types manuscripts from transcription tapes or rough-typed or handwritten copy. Experienced in formatting and interpreting editing remarks into final copy with high degree of accuracy.

Transcription Typist (60 wpm)   Formats and types a variety of correspondence, including reports, speeches, and forms. May type from drafts with two or more sources and set up forms and standard tabulations. Knowledgeable in spelling, punctuation, spacing, and syllabification. Has experience with recording tape systems, and performs other general clerical duties.

Statistical Typist (50 wpm)   Types complicated tables, business reports, tax forms, financial statements, and so forth, from drafts. Verifies figures. Uses good judgment in formatting to maintain balance and uniformity throughout material.

Specialized Typist (55 wpm)   Types accurately, but has knowledge of specialized terminology, symbols, forms, and procedures of a particular field, such as medicine, insurance, engineering, or law. Usually has moderate experience in area of specialization.

Specialized Transcription Typist (55 wpm)   Same as Specialized Typist, but also includes ability to use recording tape system.

WORD PROCESSING

Word Processor Trainee (60 wpm) Senior typist with excellent spelling and grammatical skills, who can be trained directly at client company for a specific application.

Word Processor Junior Operator From draft or pretyped copy, produces form letters using merge functions.

Word Processor Proofreader Highly accurate proofreader who checks copy against original draft or transcription tape for consistent format and correct grammar, punctuation, and spelling.

Word Processor Statistical Operator Formats and types tables or charts from drafts. Uses specialized column and decimal functions. May verify figures.

Word Processor Operator (50 wpm) Highly experienced in client's system and its applications. Produces all types of correspondence, reports, charts, manuals, and outlines in final form. Accurately proofreads against original draft or transcription tapes.

Word Processor Technical Operator (50 wpm) Highly experienced in client's system and its applications. Produces all types of correspondence, reports, charts, manuals, and outlines in final form. Possesses thorough knowledge of the forms, symbols, terminology, and procedures of a specialized field such as law, medicine, insurance, or engineering. Proofreads accurately against original rough drafts or transcription tapes.

Word Processor Transcription Operator Formats and types a variety of correspondence, including reports and speeches. May type from drafts with two or more sources. Knowledgeable in spelling.

Word Processor Secretary (60 wpm) Very experienced in a given word processor system. Sets up, prepares, and proofreads correspondence and other copy in final form. Answers and places telephone calls; files, receives and screens visitors; distributes mail; sets up appointments; and makes travel arrangements. No shorthand required.

Word Processor Transcription Secretary (60 wpm) Same as Word Processor Secretary, but is also able to operate various types of transcribing machines.

Word Processor Technical Secretary (60 wpm) Experienced secretary with thorough understanding of client's system and its applications. Produces all types of correspondence, reports, and other copy in final form from drafts. Knowledgeable in the forms, symbols, terminology, and procedures of a specialized field, such as law, medicine, insurance, or engineering. Performs general secretarial duties, such as answering telephones, distributing mail, receiving and screening visitors, making appointments and travel arrangements, and filing.

LIGHT INDUSTRIAL

Assembler—Unskilled Works as member of assembly line group. Attaches one unit to another and passes the unit along for further assembly. Can use small hand tools, such as air screwdriver or wrench. No experience required, and needs to be supervised.

Assembler—Electronic Does electrical or electronic assembly on printed circuits or chassis within a production group. This may include installing and soldering wires and components; cutting and shaping various wire materials; attaching switches, transformers, or transistors to circuit boards. May sort, test, and inspect small parts and use simple hand tools to accomplish the above. Works from blueprints, verbal instructions, wire lists, or schematic diagrams. Needs supervision.

Expediter Routes, dispatches, and distributes materials to ensure that each function within an organization has needed supplies. Handles shortages and substitutions, and generally responds to fluctuating production schedules.

Inspector Experienced in inspecting, testing, and checking parts, assemblies, and systems. May be involved in incoming inspection, manufacturing, or final testing. Can work from schematics, invoices, and layout diagrams. Maintains test records and evaluates results.

FACTORY/WAREHOUSE

Forklift Operator   Experienced in operating vehicle which loads or picks up products and materials in storage yard, warehouse, or factory. Inventories, weighs, and tags material. Employer-driver release required.

Materials Handler   Loads, unloads, and moves materials within or near work site. Stacks and labels bundles of materials for identification. Moves materials weighing up to 50 pounds by hand, hand truck, or wheelbarrow. Keeps accurate, simple records, and follows written or verbal directions well.

Janitor   Maintains premises in clean and orderly condition. May do any or all of the following: cleaning and polishing floors, walls, furniture, and fixtures; picking up refuse from ground areas and disposing of trash; setting up chairs and tables. May keep exterior areas clear of snow or ice.

Packer   Packs stock items according to client's specifications. Checks and labels items, and verifies against order or stock list.

Stock Clerk   Selects items from shelves or bins that are listed on order lists. Checks and documents list for completeness, noting out-of-stock, back-ordered, or discontinued items. Delivers items to packing room or area.

Shipping/Receiving Clerk   Verifies and records incoming and outgoing shipments. Prepares items for shipping, using cartons, containers, and protective fillers. Seals and labels cartons for proper identification, and calculates and records proper postage. Checks and examines incoming items against bills of lading, invoices, orders, or other records. Routes items to departments by hand, hand truck, or dolly. Keeps accurate records, and follows verbal and written directions well.

Packager/Sealer   Covers products in plastic, cellophane, bubble pack, or blister bags. Seals packages using glue, heat sealer, or heat tunnel.

DIRECTORY OF TEMPORARY SERVICES, BY STATE AND CITY

The following directory lists temporary employment services that are members of the National Association of Temporary Services. As mentioned at the end of Chapter 4, we recommend that you work for a service that belongs to this organization. Of course, there are many very good services that may not be members of NATS. However, all NATS member services must adhere to a certain code of ethics that gives you some protection as a temporary employee.

The organization of this directory by state and city should be useful to you if you are ever traveling and need to find temporary work away from home.

Please note that three of the largest national services do not appear in the directory. They are Kelly Services Inc., Manpower Inc., and The Olsten Corporation. For a complete listing of their offices, you may write for information at their corporate headquarters.

- Kelly Services Inc.
  999 West Big Beaver Road
  Troy, Michigan 48084

- Manpower Inc.
  5301 North Ironwood Road
  P.O. Box 2053
  Milwaukee, Wisconsin 53201
- The Olsten Corporation
  1 Merrick Avenue
  Westbury, New York 11590

Western Temporary Services and Accountemps Inc. are *not* members of NATS. However, since both of these services are nationwide, we feel it is important to offer the addresses of their corporate headquarters.

- Western Temporary Services
  301 Lennon Lane
  P.O. Box 9230
  Walnut Creek, California 94596-9280
- Accountemps Inc.
  111 Pine Street, #1500
  San Francisco, California 94111

City, State Membership Listing

ALABAMA

ANNISTON
TEMP FORCE OF ANNISTON
TEMPORARY RESOURCES INC

AUBURN
PERSONNEL CONCEPTS INC

BIRMINGHAM
ACTION STAFFING TEMP HELP DIV
ADIA PERSONNEL SERVICES
DUNHILL TEMPORARY SYSTEMS
HEALTHCARE STAFFING SVCS INC
NORRELL SERVICES
PERSONNEL POOL OF AMERICA
SNELLING & SNELLING
TEAM SERVICES INC
TEMPWORLD INC
XTRA HELPERS

DOTHAN
PERSONNEL RESOURCES

FOLEY
MULTI TEMPS

GADSDEN
CON-TEMPORARY PERSONNEL

HOOVER
TEMPWORLD INC

HUNTSVILLE
ADIA PERSONNEL SERVICES
HEALTHCARE STAFFING SVCS INC
NORRELL SERVICES
SNELLING TEMPORARIES
TEMP FORCE OF HUNTSVILLE

MOBILE
MULTI-TEMPS
PREFERRED TEMPORARY SERVICES

OPELIKA
TEMPORARY ALTERNATIVES INC

ARIZONA

CASA GRANDE
TEMP FORCE OF PINAL COUNTY

GLENDALE
ADIA PERSONNEL SERVICES

MESA
ADIA PERSONNEL SERVICES
SNELLING TEMPORARIES
VOLT TEMPORARY SERVICES

PHOENIX
ADIA PERSONNEL SERVICES
BANNER TEMPORARY SERVICES
DARLENE RIED TEMPORARIES INC
DATA REGISTRY INC
PEAKLOAD SERVICES
PERSONNEL POOL OF AMERICA
SNELLING TEMPORARIES
STAFF BUILDERS
STAFF TEMPS INC
STIVERS TEMPORARY PERSONNEL
TEMPORARIES INC
VOLT TEMPORARY SERVICES

SCOTTSDALE
NORRELL SERVICES
TEMPORARIES INC
TEMPORARY TECHS OF ARIZONA INC

TEMPE
ADIA PERSONNEL SERVICES
HOURS INC
PERSONNEL POOL OF AMERICA
STAFF BUILDERS
TRANSWORLD TEMPORARIES
UNIFORCE TEMPORARY SERVICES

TUCSON
ADIA PERSONNEL SERVICES
ALICE & MARY'S TEMPORARY SVCS
CAMERON & COMPANY
EXPRESS SERVICES INC
K-TEMP TEMPORARY SERVICES
NORRELL SERVICES
PERSONNEL POOL OF AMERICA
SNELLING TEMPORARIES
VOLT TEMPORARY SERVICES

ARKANSAS

FORT SMITH
EXPRESS SERVICES INC
TEC, THE EMPLOYMENT COMPANY
TEMP FORCE OF FORT SMITH

LITTLE ROCK
ADIA PERSONNEL SERVICES
DUNHILL TEMPORARY SYSTEMS
PERSONNEL POOL OF AMERICA
SNELLING TEMPORARIES

NORTH LITTLE ROCK
DUNHILL TEMPORARY SYSTEMS
EXPRESS SERVICES INC

PINE BLUFF
EXPRESS SERVICES INC
TEMP FORCE—PINE BLUFF AR

RUSSELLVILLE
EXPRESS SERVICES INC

SCOTTSDALE
TALENT TREE

SPRINGDALE
EXPRESS SERVICES INC

CALIFORNIA

ANAHEIM
ADIA PERSONNEL SERVICES
ITT EMPLOYER SERVICES
NORRELL SERVICES
OFFICE SPECIALISTS
UNIFORCE TEMPORARY SERVICES
UNITED TEMPORARY SERVICES INC
VOLT TEMPORARY SERVICES

ARCADIA
COURTESY TEMPORARY SERVICE INC
NORRELL SERVICES

BAKERSFIELD
PERSONNEL POOL OF AMERICA
VOLT TEMPORARY SERVICES

BERKELEY
ADIA PERSONNEL SERVICES
ITT EMPLOYER SERVICES INC

BEVERLY HILLS
ITT EMPLOYER SERVICES
MAYDAY TEMPORARY PERSONNEL
TEMP FORCE OF BEVERLY HILLS
UNIFORCE TEMPORARY SERVICES

BREA
ABIGAIL ABBOTT TEMPORARIES
HELPMATES PERSONNEL SERVICES
NORRELL SERVICES
TALENT TREE TEMPORARIES
UNITED TEMPORARY SERVICES INC

BURBANK
ACTIVE TEMPORARY SERVICES
VOLT TEMPORARY SERVICES

BURLINGAME
MORTGAGE PROFESSIONALS, THE

This listing reflects member office locations as reported by each headquarters company member.

CAMARILLO
ABACUS TEMPS

CAMPBELL
CERTIFIED FLEXSTAFF

CANOGA PARK
VALLEY TEMPS INC

CAPITOLA
NORRELL SERVICES

CARLSBAD
ADIA PERSONNEL SERVICES
VOLT TEMPORARY SERVICES

CARSON
NORRELL SERVICES

CERRITOS
ABIGAIL ABBOTT TEMPORARIES
ACCOUNTANTS OVERLOAD
ADIA PERSONNEL SERVICES
PERSONNEL POOL OF AMERICA
VOLT TEMPORARY SERVICES

CHICO
EXPRESS SERVICES INC

CITRUS HEIGHTS
ADIA PERSONNEL SERVICES
EXPRESS SERVICES INC

CITY OF INDUSTRY
ACCOUNTANTS OVERLOAD

CONCORD
OFFICE SPECIALISTS
PACIFIC MEDICAL CARE INC
TEMPORARY SKILLS UNLIMITED INC

CORONA
CORONA TEMPORARIES

CORONA DEL MAR
ARHNESS COVENTRY INC

COSTA MESA
ACCOUNTANTS OVERLOAD
ADIA PERSONNEL SERVICES
ITT EMPLOYER SERVICES
UNIFORCE OF COSTA MESA

COVINA
ADIA PERSONNEL SERVICES
NORRELL SERVICES
OLYMPIC TEMPORARY
  SERVICES/PROFORCE
  TEMPORARIES INC
PERSONNEL POOL OF AMERICA

STAFF BUILDERS
VOLT TEMPORARY SERVICES

CULVER CITY
ADIA PERSONNEL SERVICES

CUPERTINO
ADIA PERSONNEL SERVICES

CYPRESS
NORRELL SERVICES

DOWNEY
ADIA PERSONNEL SERVICES
UNITED TEMPORARY SERVICES INC
VOLT TEMPORARY SERVICES

DUBLIN
OFFICE SPECIALISTS
PERSONNEL POOL OF AMERICA
STAFF BUILDERS

ENCINO
ADIA PERSONNEL SERVICES
ITT EMPLOYER SERVICES
TRANSWORLD TEMPORARIES
UNITED TEMPORARY SERVICES INC
VOLT TEMPORARY SERVICES

FAIR OAKS
ROBERTA'S TEMPORARY SERVICE
TRANSWORLD TEMPORARIES

FAIRFIELD
ADIA PERSONNEL SERVICES
EXPRESS SERVICES INC

FOUNTAIN VALLEY
COURTESY TEMPORARY SERVICE INC
HELPMATES PERSONNEL SERVICES

FREMONT
ADIA PERSONNEL SERVICES
OFFICE SPECIALISTS
PERSONNEL POOL OF AMERICA
ROBERTA'S TEMPORARY SERVICE
UNIFORCE TEMPORARY SERVICES

FRESNO
ADIA PERSONNEL SERVICES
AMERICAN TEMPORARY SERVICES
DENHAM TEMPORARY SERVICES
NORRELL SERVICES
PERSONNEL POOL OF AMERICA
SNELLING TEMPORARIES
VOLT TEMPORARY SERVICES

GLENDALE
ADIA PERSONNEL SERVICES
CDI TEMPORARY SERVICES
UNITED TEMPORARY SERVICES INC

GLENDORA
COURTESY TEMPORARY SERVICE INC

HACIENDA HEIGHTS
COURTESY TEMPORARY SERVICE INC
TRANSWORLD TEMPORARIES

HAYWARD
ADIA PERSONNEL SERVICES
CERTIFIED FLEXSTAFF
PERSONNEL POOL OF AMERICA
SNELLING TEMPORARIES
STAFF BUILDERS
VOLT TEMPORARY SERVICES

IRVINE
AUBREY THOMAS TEMPORARIES
NEWPORT TEMPORARIES INC
NORRELL SERVICES
TEMP ASSOCIATES
TEMPORARIES INC
VICKI HESTON PERSONNEL SERVICES
  INC

LA MESA
TEMP FORCE OF SAN DIEGO
VOLT TEMPORARY SERVICES

LAGUNA HILLS
ADIA PERSONNEL SERVICES
ITT EMPLOYER SERVICES INC

LAKEWOOD
NORRELL SERVICES

LONG BEACH
ABIGAIL ABBOTT TEMPORARIES
ADIA PERSONNEL SERVICES
STAFF BUILDERS
UNIFORCE TEMPORARY SERVICES
UNITED TEMPORARY SERVICES INC
VOLT TEMPORARY SERVICES

LOS ALAMITOS
EXPRESS SERVICES INC

LOS ANGELES
ACCOUNTANTS OVERLOAD
ADIA PERSONNEL SERVICES
METRO TEMPORARY SERVICES
NORRELL SERVICES
OXFORD & ASSOCIATES INC
PERSONNEL POOL OF AMERICA
STAFF BUILDERS
STIVERS TEMPORARY PERSONNEL
SYSTEMP
TEMPORARIES INC
TEMPORARY CENTER USA CORP
TRANSWORLD TEMPORARIES INC
TRC TEMPORARY SERVICES INC
UNITED TEMPORARY SERVICES INC
VOLT TEMPORARY SERVICES

MARINA DEL REY
TEMP-LINE SERVICES

MENLO PARK
ADIA TEMPORARY SERVICES

MISSION VIEJO
UNITED TEMPORARY SERVICES INC
VOLT TEMPORARY SERVICE INC

MODESTO
ADIA PERSONNEL SERVICES
PERSONNEL POOL OF AMERICA
PRN SERVICES INC

MONTCLAIR
PERSONNEL POOL OF AMERICA

MONTEREY
SNELLING TEMPORARIES

MOUNTAIN VIEW
ADIA PERSONNEL SERVICES
CERTIFIED FLEXSTAFF
OXFORD & ASSOCIATES INC

NAPA
NELSON PERSONNEL SERVICES

NEWPORT BEACH
ABIGAIL ABBOTT TEMPORARIES
ADIA PERSONNEL SERVICES
NORRELL SERVICES
TRC TEMPORARY SERVICES INC
UNITED TEMPORARY SERVICES INC
VOLT TEMPORARY SERVICES

NORTH HOLLYWOOD
ADIA PERSONNEL SERVICES
ESCROW OVERLAND

NORWALK
ESP PERSONNEL SERVICES

OAKLAND
ADIA PERSONNEL SERVICES
CERTIFIED FLEXSTAFF
STAFF BUILDERS
VOLT TEMPORARY SERVICES

OCEANSIDE
STAFF BUILDERS

ORANGE
ADIA PERSONNEL SERVICES
STAFF BUILDERS
VOLT TEMPORARY SERVICES

OXNARD
PERSONNEL POOL OF AMERICA
VOLT TEMPORARY SERVICES

PALM DESERT
NORRELL SERVICES
SOUTHERN TEMPORARY SERVICES

PALM SPRINGS
SOUTHERN TEMPORARY SERVICES

PALO ALTO
ADIA PERSONNEL SERVICES
PERSONNEL POOL OF AMERICA
Q TECH
ROBERTA'S TEMPORARY SERVICE
SNELLING TEMPORARIES

PASADENA
ACCOUNTANTS OVERLOAD
ADIA PERSONNEL SERVICES
ITT EMPLOYER SERVICES
STIVERS TEMPORARIES PERSONNEL
VOLT TEMPORARY SERVICES

PLACENTIA
NORRELL SERVICES

PLEASANT HILL
ADIA PERSONNEL SERVICES
NELSON PERSONNEL SERVICES

PLEASANTON
SNELLING TEMPORARIES
TEMPORARY SKILLS UNLIMITED

RANCHO CORDOVA
DUNHILL TEMPORARY SYSTEMS

RANCHO CUCAMONGA
ADIA PERSONNEL SERVICES
CDI TEMPORARY SERVICES INC
UNITED TEMPORARY SERVICES INC

REDDING
EXPRESS SERVICES INC

REDONDO BEACH
SAWYER & ASSOCIATES

RIDGECREST
SECRETARIAL AND ADMINISTRATIVE
    SUPPORT SERVICES (SASS)
T.O.S.S. TEMPORARIES

RIVERSIDE
ADIA PERSONNEL SERVICES
CDI TEMPORARY SERVICES INC
UNIFORCE OF RIVERSIDE CA
VOLT TEMPORARY SERVICES

ROLLING HILLS
CAMERON & COMPANY

ROSEVILLE
DUNHILL TEMPORARY SYSTEMS

SACRAMENTO
ACTION TEMPS INC
ADIA PERSONNEL SERVICES
CAL TEMPS
CERTIFIED FLEXSTAFF
NORRELL SERVICES
PERSONNEL POOL OF AMERICA
Q TECH
RITZ TEMPORARY SERVICES
STAFF BUILDERS
TEMPEOPLE INC
UNIFORCE TEMPORARY SERVICES
VOLT TEMPORARY SERVICES

SAN BERNARDINO
STAFF BUILDERS

SAN BRUNO
ADIA PERSONNEL SERVICES
PERSONNEL POOL OF AMERICA

SAN DIEGO
ADIA PERSONNEL SERVICES
DUNHILL TEMPORARY SYSTEMS
EXPRESS SERVICES INC
GEORGIA'S TEMPORARY PERSONNEL
LAWTON COMPANY INC, THE
NORRELL SERVICES
NURSES NETWORK INC
OFFICE SPECIALISTS
OMEGA TEMPORARIES
SNELLING TEMPORARIES
STAFF BUILDERS
TEMPRO SERVICES
TOPS*
UNIFORCE TEMPORARY SERVICES
VOLT TEMPORARY SERVICES

SAN FRANCISCO
ADIA PERSONNEL SERVICES
AMERICAN STAFFING COMPANY
BENTLEY TEMPORARIES
CERTIFIED FLEXSTAFF
DUNHILL TEMPORARY SYSTEMS
GALLAGHER STAFFING ASSOCIATES
ITT EMPLOYER SERVICES
LONA JENSEN TEMPORARY SERVICES
NELSON PERSONNEL SERVICES
NORRELL SERVICES
OFFICE SPECIALISTS
PEOPLE CONNECTION INC, THE
PERSONNEL POOL OF AMERICA
Q TECH
RESOURCE TEMPORARY SERVICE
STAFF BUILDERS
TEMP FORCE OF SAN FRANCISCO
TEMP-O-RAMA TEMPORARY
    SERVICES
TEMPORARIES INC
TEMPORARIES NETWORK
TEMPOSITIONS INC
UNIFORCE TEMPORARY SERVICES

VOLT TEMPORARY SERVICES

SAN GABRIEL
UNITED TEMPORARY SERVICES INC

SAN JOSE
ADIA PERSONNEL SERVICES
ASAP TEMPORARY ACCOUNTING
   PERSONNEL SERVICE INC
CONTEMPORARIES OF SANTA CLARA
   COUNTY INC
CONTROL DATA TEMPS
Q TECH
RESOURCE PERSONNEL SERVICES
SNELLING TEMPORARIES
STAFF BUILDERS

SAN JUAN CAPISTRANO
REMEDY TEMPORARY SERVICES

SAN MARCOS
ADIA PERSONNEL SERVICES
DUNHILL TEMPORARY SYSTEMS
VOLT TEMPORARY SERVICES

SAN MATEO
ACCOUNTANTS INC
ADIA PERSONNEL SERVICES
PERSONNEL POOL OF AMERICA
ROBERTA'S TEMPORARY SERVICE
TEMP FORCE OF SAN MATEO
TOD TEMPORARY SERVICES

SAN RAFAEL
CAMERON & COMPANY
NELSON PERSONNEL SERVICES

SAN RAMON
ADIA PERSONNEL SERVICES
Q TECH

SANTA ANA
ADIA PERSONNEL SERVICES
HELPMATES PERSONNEL SERVICES
NORRELL SERVICES
OFFICE SPECIALISTS
TAD TECHNICAL SERVICES CORP
TRC TEMPORARY SERVICES INC
VOLT TEMPORARY SERVICES

SANTA BARBARA
SNELLING TEMPORARIES
TEMP FORCE OF SANTA BARBARA
VOLT TEMPORARY SERVICES

SANTA CLARA
ARROWSTAFF TEMPORARY SERVICES
BEST TEMPORARY SERVICES
OXFORD & ASSOCIATES INC
PERSONNEL POOL OF AMERICA
Q TECH
ROBERTA'S TEMPORARY SERVICE

SANTA FE SPRINGS
HELPMATES PERSONNEL SERVICES

SANTA MARIA
VOLT TEMPORARY SERVICES
WALTEK

SANTA ROSA
PERSONNEL POOL OF AMERICA

SHERMAN OAKS
NORRELL SERVICES
STAFF BUILDERS

SIMI VALLEY
CDI TEMPORARY SERVICES INC
VOLT TEMPORARY SERVICES

SO SAN FRANCISCO
SNELLING TEMPORARIES

STOCKTON
ADIA PERSONNEL SERVICES
ICS TEMPORARY SERVICES
NORRELL SERVICES
PERSONNEL POOL OF AMERICA
UNIFORCE TEMPORARY SERVICES

SUMMYVALE
ADIA PERSONNEL SERVICES

TARZANA
KIMBALL GROUP PERSONNEL SVC
TEMP FORCE—SAN FERNANDO VLY

TEMPLE CITY
CDI TEMPORARY SERVICES INC

THOUSAND OAKS
ADIA PERSONNEL SERVICES
CHRISTOPHER & ASSOCIATES
   TEMPORARY SERVICES
VOLT TEMPORARY SERVICES

TORRANCE
ACCOUNTANTS OVERLOAD
ADIA PERSONNEL SERVICES
CDI TEMPORARY SERVICES INC
HELPMATES PERSONNEL SERVICES
ITT EMPLOYER SERVICES
NORRELL SERVICES
PAT SERVICES INC
TRANSWORLD TEMPORARIES
UNITED TEMPORARY SERVICES INC
VOLT TEMPORARY SERVICES

TUSTIN
ABIGAIL ABBOTT TEMPORARIES
PERSONNEL POOL OF AMERICA
SNELLING TEMPORARIES
TOPS TEMPORARIES

UNITED TEMPORARY SERVICES INC

UPLAND
SNELLING TEMPORARIES
VOLT TEMPORARY SERVICES

VACAVILLE
EXPRESS SERVICES INC

VAN NUYS
ADIA PERSONNEL SERVICES
TAD TECHNICAL SERVICES CORP

VENTURA
CDI TEMPORARY SERVICES INC
STAFF BUILDERS

VISALIA
ADIA PERSONNEL SERVICES
PERSONNEL POOL OF AMERICA
TEMP FORCE OF VISALIA

WALNUT CREEK
ADIA PERSONNEL SERVICES
DUNHILL TEMPORARY SYSTEMS
NORRELL SERVICES
PERSONNEL POOL OF AMERICA
SNELLING TEMPORARIES
STAFF BUILDERS
TEMPORARY SKILLS UNLIMITED INC
TEMPOSITIONS INC
VOLT TEMPORARY SERVICES

WEST COVINA
UNITED TEMPORARY SERVICES INC

WEST LAKE VILLAGE
PERSONNEL POOL OF AMERICA

WEST LOS ANGELES
WORK CENTER INC

WESTLAKE VILLAGE
CDI TEMPORARY SERVICES INC

WOODLAND
ADIA PERSONNEL SERVICES

WOODLAND HILLS
ACCOUNTANTS OVERLOAD
ADIA PERSONNEL SERVICES
CDI TEMPORARY SERVICES INC

YUBA CITY
EXPRESS SERVICES INC

COLORADO

AURORA
EXPRESS SERVICES INC
NORRELL SERVICES
OFFICE SPECIALISTS

VOLT TEMPORARY SERVICES

BOULDER

ADIA PERSONNEL SERVICES
EXPRESS SERVICES INC

COLORADO SPRINGS

ADD STAFF INC
ADIA PERSONNEL SERVICES
ARROW AND AND-EX TEMPORARY
  HELP
EXPRESS SERVICES INC
SNELLING TEMPORARIES
SOS TEMPORARY SERVICES

DENVER

ADIA PERSONNEL SERVICES
J KENT TEMPORARIES
NORRELL SERVICES
PERSONNEL POOL OF AMERICA
TEMP FORCE OF DENVER
TEMPORARIES INC
TEMPORARY ACCOUNTING
  PERSONNEL OF COLORADO INC
THE TEMPORARY WORKS INC
TOPS*
VOLT TEMPORARY SERVICES

ENGLEWOOD

ADIA PERSONNEL SERVICES
NORRELL SERVICES
PATTERNS INC
PEAKLOAD SERVICES
TALENT TREE TEMPORARIES
TOPS*

FORT COLLINS

EXPRESS SERVICES INC
NORRELL SERVICES

GRAND JUNCTION

SOS TEMPORARY SERVICES

GREELEY

EXPRESS SERVICES INC

LONGMONT

EXPRESS SERVICES INC

LOVELAND

EXPRESS SERVICES INC
ON CALL TEMPORARY SERVICES

PUEBLO

EXPRESS SERVICES INC
TEMP FORCE OF PUEBLO

WESTMINSTER

EXPRESS SERVICES INC
OFFICE SPECIALISTS

CONNECTICUT

BRIDGEPORT

DUNHILL TEMPORARY SYSTEMS
TRACY TEMPORARIES INC

DANBURY

DUNHILL TEMPORARY SYSTEMS
QUALITY PERSONNEL SERVICES
SNELLING TEMPORARIES
TEMPS, INC

DARIEN

SOUND TEMPORARIES

EAST HARTFORD

DUNHILL TEMPORARY SYSTEMS
JOBPRO TEMPORARY SERVICES INC

EAST WINDSOR

DUNHILL TEMPORARY SYSTEMS

FAIRFIELD

OFFICE SERVICES OF CT INC

FARMINGTON

DUNHILL TEMPORARY SYSTEMS
NORRELL SERVICES

HAMDEN

NORRELL SERVICES

HARTFORD

ACCOUNTING FUTURES INC
ADIA PERSONNEL SERVICES
CENTURY TEMPORARIES
CO-OPPORTUNITY PERSONNEL
  SERVICES INC
HALLMARK TEMPS INC
J. MORRISSEY & COMPANY
MERRY EMPLOYMENT GROUP INC
NORRELL SERVICES
TEMP FORCE OF HARTFORD
TEMPBUREAU INC
UNIFORCE TEMPORARY SERVICES

MILFORD

LABOR FORCE OF AMERICA

NEW HAVEN

ADIA PERSONNEL SERVICES
DIVERSIFIED EMPLOYMENT SERVICES
  INC
DUNHILL TEMPORARY SYSTEMS
JACKIE MATCHETT TEMPORARY SVCS
PERSONNEL POOL OF AMERICA
TRACY TEMPORARIES INC

NEWINGTON

OLSTEN TEMPORARY SERVICES

NORWALK

AUBREY THOMAS TEMPORARIES
SNELLING TEMPORARIES

NORWICH

PERSONNEL POOL OF AMERICA

SHELTON

DIVERSIFIED EMPLOYMENT SVCS

SOUTHINGTON

CENTURY TEMPORARIES
TEMP FORCE OF HARTFORD II

STAMFORD

ADIA PERSONNEL SERVICES
ADVANTAGE INC
AMTEMP
AUBREY THOMAS TEMPORARIES
CONNECTICUT TEMPORARIES INC
COSMOPOLITAN CARE CORPORATION
DIANA OFFICE TEMPS
HUMAN RESOURCE TEMPS INC
NORRELL SERVICES
PERSONNEL POOL OF AMERICA
TEMP FORCE OF STAMFORD

STRATFORD

HUMAN RESOURCE TEMPS INC
MK TEMPORARY SERVICES INC
OFFICE SERVICES OF CT INC

TRUMBULL

OFFICE SERVICES OF CT INC

WALLINGFORD

DUNHILL TEMPORARY SYSTEMS

WATERBURY

JACI CARROLL PERSONNEL SERVICES
  INC
MANPOWER TEMPORARY SERVICES

WEST HARTFORD

JBS INC

WILTON

PATHFINDER GROUP INC

WINDSOR

SNELLING TEMPORARIES

DELAWARE

WILMINGTON

BSI TEMPORARIES OF DELAWARE INC
CALDWELL TEMPORARY SERVICES
CDI TEMPORARY SERVICES INC
COMPUTER RELATED TEMPORARIES
NORRELL SERVICES
PERSONNEL POOL OF AMERICA
STAR TEMPS INC

DISTRICT OF COLUMBIA

WASHINGTON

ADIA PERSONNEL SERVICES
ADVANTAGE INC
AMERITEMPS INC

AUTOMATED INFORMATION
   MANAGEMENT INC
COMPETEMPS BY DORA INC
CUP TEMPORARIES INC
DURHAM TEMPORARIES INC
GOODFRIEND TEMPORARY SERVICES
HOSPITAL TEMPORARIES
HOSPITAL/HOME CARE TEMPORARIES
   INC
INGRID'S TEMPS
INTERSEC PERSONNEL SERVICE
JEANE HALE TEMPORARIES
LEGAL ASSISTANTS CORP
NORRELL SERVICES
PERSONNEL POOL OF AMERICA
SNELLING TEMPORARIES
STAFF BUILDERS
STAFF SEARCH TEMPS
SYSTEMS SUPPORT CORPORATION
T.H.E. ACCOUNTING TEMPORARIES
TAD TECHNICAL SERVICES CORP
TALENT TREE TEMPORARIES
TELE SEC TEMPORARY SERVICES
TEMPO STAFF OF AMERICA INC
TEMPORARIES INC
TEMPORARY RESOURCES
TODAYS TEMPORARIES
TRACY TEMPORARIES INC
UNIFORCE TEMPORARY
   SERVICES/POLLY FIELDS
   TEMPORARY SVCS
WOODSIDE EMPLOYMENT
   CONSULTANTS INC

FLORIDA

ALTAMONTE SPRINGS
TEMP FORCE OF ALTAMONTE
   SPRINGS

BOCA RATON
DAVID WOOD TEMPORARIES
NORRELL SERVICES
OFFICE SPECIALISTS
TRACY TEMPORARIES INC

BRADENTON
T.O.P.S. TEMPS OF MANATEE
TEMP CAREERS INC

BRANDON
ACTION STAFFING TEMPORARY HELP
   DIVISION
ADIA PERSONNEL SERVICES
NORRELL SERVICES

CLEARWATER
ABLEST SERVICES CORPORATION
STAFF BUILDERS
UNIFORCE TEMPORARY SERVICES

CORALS GABLES
SOC TEMPORARY SERVICES

DAYTONA BEACH
DAYTONA TEMPORARY STAFFING INC
NORRELL SERVICES
TODAYS TEMPORARIES

DEERFIELD
PERSONNEL POOL OF AMERICA

DELRAY BEACH
ADIA PERSONNEL SERVICES
PERSONNEL POOL OF AMERICA

FERNANDINA BEACH
JBS INC

FORT LAUDERDALE
ADIA PERSONNEL SERVICES
ASSOCIATED TEMPORARY STAFFING
   INC
DAVID WOOD TEMPORARIES
JBS INC
NORRELL SERVICES
PEAKLOAD SERVICES
PERSONNEL POOL OF AMERICA
PREMIER SERVICES INC
SNELLING TEMPORARIES
STAFF BUILDERS
TRACY TEMPORARIES INC
TRC TEMPORARY SERVICES INC

FORT MYERS
ADIA PERSONNEL SERVICES
NORRELL SERVICES
PERSONNEL POOL OF AMERICA
PERSONNEL SERVICES OF FT MYERS
   INC
SNELLING TEMPORARIES

FORT PIERCE
JBS INC

GAINESVILLE
NORRELL SERVICES
PERSONNEL POOL OF AMERICA
TEMP FORCE OF GAINESVILLE

HIALEAH
OFFICE SPECIALISTS

HOLLY HILL
ADIA PERSONNEL SERVICES

INVERNESS
PERSONNEL POOL OF AMERICA

JACKSONVILLE
ABLEST SERVICES CORPORATION
ADIA PERSONNEL SERVICES
ASSOCIATED TEMPORARY STAFFING
   INC
CDI TEMPORARY SERVICES INC
EXPRESS SERVICES INC

HOURS INC
JBS INC
NORRELL SERVICES
PERSONNEL POOL OF AMERICA
TEAM SERVICES INC
TEMPORARIES INC
TODAYS TEMPORARIES
TRACY TEMPORARIES INC

JACKSONVILLE BEACH
JBS INC

JUPITER
OFFICE PERSONNEL PLUS

KEY WEST
GIRL FRIDAY, THE

KISSIMMEE
PERSONNEL POOL OF AMERICA

LAKE WORTH
PERSONNEL POOL OF AMERICA

LAKELAND
NORRELL SERVICES

LARGO
DUNHILL TEMPORARY SYSTEMS OF
   ST PETERSBURG
EPIC PERSONNEL SERVICES

LAUDERDALE LAKES
UNIFORCE TEMPORARY SERVICES

LEESBURG
NORRELL SERVICES
T.O.P.S. TEMPS

MAITLAND
SNELLING TEMPORARIES
TODAYS TEMPORARIES

MARGATE
OFFICE SPECIALISTS

MELBOURNE
NORRELL SERVICES

MIAMI
ADIA PERSONNEL SERVICES
ADVANTAGE PERSONNEL AGENCY INC
CREATIVE STAFFING
DAVID WOOD TEMPORARIES
HASTINGS & HASTINGS TEMPORARY
   SERVICES INC
LINDA ROBINS & ASSOCIATES INC
NORRELL SERVICES
OFFICE SPECIALISTS
PERSONNEL POOL OF AMERICA
QUALITY FIRST MORTGAGE PROS

STAR TEMPS/STAR NATIONAL INC
TODAYS TEMPORARIES
TRACY TEMPORARIES INC
TRC TEMPORARY SERVICES INC

MIAMI LAKES
ADIA PERSONNEL SERVICES
NORRELL SERVICES

NAPLES
PERSONNEL POOL OF AMERICA

NORTH MIAMI
ADIA PERSONNEL SERVICES
OFFICE SPECIALISTS
SOC TEMPORARY SERVICES

NORTH MIAMI BEACH
DUNHILL TEMPORARY SYSTEMS
TRACY TEMPORARIES INC

NORTH PALM BEACH
NORRELL SERVICES

OAKLAND PARK
TODAYS TEMPORARIES
TRACY TEMPORARIES INC

OCALA
NORRELL SERVICES
PERSONNEL POOL OF AMERICA

ORANGE PARK
ACTION STAFFING TEMPORARY HELP
   DIVISION

ORLANDO
ABLEST SERVICES CORPORATION
ADIA PERSONNEL SERVICES
ASSOCIATED TEMPORARY STAFFING
   INC
COSMOPOLITAN CARE CORPORATION
JBS INC
NORRELL SERVICES
PERSONNEL POOL OF AMERICA
STAFF BUILDERS
TEAM SERVICES INC
TEMPORARIES INC
TEMPORARY SERVICES INC
TRACY TEMPORARIES INC
TRANSWORLD TEMPORARIES

PALM HARBOR
ADIA PERSONNEL SERVICES
CROWN PERSONNEL SERVICES INC

PENSACOLA
LANDRUM TEMPORARY SERVICES
PERSONNEL POOL OF AMERICA
PREFERRED TEMPORARY SERVICES

PINELLAS PARK
PERSONNEL POOL OF AMERICA

PLANTATION
OFFICE SPECIALISTS
STAFF PLANNING INC

POMPANO BEACH
TRACY TEMPORARIES INC
XTRA HELPERS

PORT SAINT LUCIE
PERSONNEL PLUS INC

RIVIERA BEACH
PEAKLOAD SERVICES

SAINT PETERSBURG
ACTION STAFFING TEMPORARY HELP
   DIVISION
ADIA PERSONNEL SERVICES
COMPUTERPEOPLE INC
SNELLING TEMPORARIES

SARASOTA
ADIA PERSONNEL SERVICES
EAST-WEST TEMPORARIES INC
NORRELL SERVICES
PERSONNEL POOL OF AMERICA
SNELLING TEMPORARIES
T.O.P.S. TEMPS

SOUTH MIAMI
OFFICE SPECIALISTS

SUNRISE
NORRELL SERVICES
TEAM SERVICES INC
TODAYS TEMPORARIES

TALLAHASSEE
NORRELL SERVICES

TAMPA
ACTION STAFFING TEMPORARY HELP
   DIVISION
ADIA PERSONNEL SERVICES
ASSOCIATED TEMPORARY STAFFING
   INC
CDI TEMPORARY SERVICES INC
EXPRESS SERVICES INC
GALE PORTER TEMPORARY
   SERVICES
HALLMARK TEMPORARIES INC
NORRELL SERVICES
OFFICE SPECIALISTS
OMEGA TEMPORARIES
PERSONNEL POOL OF AMERICA
PRO IMAGE TEMPORARIES INC
SNELLING TEMPORARIES
SOURCE ONE STAFFING INC
STAFF BUILDERS
TEMPORARIES INC
TEMPWORLD INC
TODAYS TEMPORARIES
TRACY TEMPORARIES INC

TRC TEMPORARY SERVICES INC

TAVARES
PERSONNEL POOL OF AMERICA

TEQUESTA
ADIA PERSONNEL SERVICES

VENICE
T.O.P.S. TEMPS

WEST JACKSONVILLE
JBS INC

WEST PALM BEACH
ADIA PERSONNEL SERVICES
CDI TEMPORARY SERVICES INC
DAVID WOOD TEMPORARIES
JBS INC
PERSONNEL POOL OF AMERICA
SNELLING TEMPORARIES
TEMP FORCE OF WEST PALM BEACH
TEMPORARIES INC
TRACY TEMPORARIES INC

WINTER PARK
NORRELL SERVICES
TEMPWORLD INC
TRACY TEMPORARIES INC
TRC TEMPORARY SERVICES INC
TREND TEMPORARY SERVICES

GEORGIA

ALBANY
NORRELL SERVICES

ATHENS
BOS TEMPORARIES

ATLANTA
ACTION STAFFING TEMP HELP DIV
ADIA PERSONNEL SERVICES
ASSOCIATED TEMPORARY STAFFING
   INC
CDI TEMPORARY SERVICES INC
COSMOPOLITAN CARE CORPORATION
DUNHILL TEMPORARY SYSTEMS
DURHAM TEMPORARIES INC
INTERNATIONAL INSURANCE
   PERSONNEL INC
KELLY SERVICES
LAWSTAF INC
NORRELL SERVICES
PEAKLOAD SERVICES
PERSONNEL POOL OF AMERICA
PREFERRED TEMPORARY SERVICES
SNELLING TEMPORARIES
STAFF BUILDERS
SYSTEMP
TALENT TREE TEMPORARIES
TEAM SERVICES INC
TEMP FORCE INC

TEMPORARIES INC
TEMPORARIES NETWORK
TEMPS & CO
TEMPWORLD INC
TODAYS TEMPORARIES
TOPS TEMPORARY PERSONNEL SVCS
TRC TEMPORARY SERVICES INC
TURNER TEMPORARY SERVICES
VOLT TEMPORARY SERVICES

AUGUSTA
MR/MS TEMPS
SIZEMORE PERSONNEL SVCS INC

CHAMBLEE
PERSONNEL POOL OF AMERICA

COLLEGE PARK
TEAM SERVICES INC
TEMPORARY SPECIALITIES INC

COLUMBUS
NORRELL SERVICES
PERSONNEL CONCEPTS INC
TEMPORARY ALTERNATIVES INC

CONYERS
NORRELL SERVICES
TEAM SERVICES INC

CUMBERLAND
UNIFORCE TEMPORARY SERVICES

DECATUR
NORRELL SERVICES
SNELLING TEMPORARIES

DULUTH
TEMPS & CO
TEMPWORLD INC

EAST POINT
SIMMONS TEMPORARY SERVICES INC

FORT OGLETHORPE
TAG HEALTHCARE STAFFING INC

FULTON
PERSONNEL POOL OF AMERICA

GAINESVILLE
ETCON INC
STAR TEMPS INCORPORATED

JONESBORO
TEMPWORLD INC
TRC TEMPORARY SERVICES INC

LAGRANGE
PERSONEL CONCEPTS INC

LAWRENCEVILLE
NORRELL SERVICES

LITHIA SPRINGS
NORRELL SERVICES

MACON
EMPLOYMENT MATCHMAKERS INC
NORRELL SERVICES

MARIETTA
CALDWELL TEMPORARY SERVICES
NORRELL SERVICES
PREFERRED TEMPORARY SERVICES
TODAYS TEMPORARIES
TRC TEMPORARY SERVICES INC

MARTINEZ
NORRELL SERVICES
PERSONNEL POOL OF AMERICA

MONROE
TEAM SERVICES INC

MORROW
PERSONNEL POOL OF AMERICA

NEWNAN
HELP SERVICES INC

NORCROSS
ASSOCIATED TEMPORARY STAFFING
  INC
DURHAM TEMPORARIES INC
NORRELL SERVICES
TEAM SERVICES INC
TEMPS & CO
TRC TEMPORARY SERVICES INC
VOLT TEMPORARY SERVICES

PEACHTREE CITY
PEACHTREE TEMPORARIES INC

ROSWELL
TEMPS & CO
TEMPWORLD INC
TRC TEMPORARY SERVICES INC

SAVANNAH
JBS INC
NORRELL SERVICES
PERSONNEL POOL OF AMERICA
TEMPO INC
TRC TEMPORARY SERVICES INC

SMYRNA
SNELLING TEMPORARIES
TEMPS & CO
TRC TEMPORARY SERVICES INC

THOMPSON
MR/MS TEMPS

TUCKER
CDI TEMPORARY SERVICES INC
DURHAM TEMPORARIES INC
TEAM SERVICES INC
TRC TEMPORARY SERVICES INC

VALDOSTA
NORRELL SERVICES

VILLA RICA
NORRELL SERVICES

HAWAII

HILO
UNIFORCE TEMPORARY SERVICES

HONOLULU
ADIA PERSONNEL SERVICES
DUNHILL TEMPORARY SYSTEMS
KAHU MALAMA NURSES INC
PERSONNEL POOL OF AMERICA
STRICTLY PROFESSIONAL

KAILUA-KONA
DUNHILL TEMPORARY SYSTEMS

KEALAKEKUA
UNIFORCE TEMPORARY SERVICES

KONA
PERSONNEL POOL OF AMERICA

LIHUE
PERSONNEL POOL OF AMERICA

IDAHO

BOISE
ARROW AND AND-EX TEMPORARY
  HELP
EXPRESS SERVICES INC
PROSTAFF TEMPORARY SERVICES

LEWISTON
EXPRESS SERVICES INC

ILLINOIS

ALTON
AVAILABILITY INC

ARLINGTON HEIGHTS
ADIA PERSONNEL SERVICES

AURORA
ADIA PERSONNEL SERVICES
STIVERS TEMPORARY PERSONNEL
WHITE COLLAR SERVICES

BUFFALO GROVE
ALLSTAFF SERVICES

CAROL STREAM
TAD TECHNICAL SERVICES CORP

CHAMPAIGN
NORRELL SERVICES

CHICAGO
A-PRO TEMPORARIES INC
ADIA PERSONNEL SERVICES
CDI TEMPORARY SERVICES INC
DUNHILL TEMPORARY SYSTEMS
GOOD WORKERS INC
GRAY PERSONNEL SERVICES
HELPMATE INC
KLATT EMPLOYMENT SERVICE INC
LASALLE SERVICES LTD
N.J.W. OFFICE PERSONNEL
NORRELL SERVICES
OLSTEN TEMPORARY SERVICES
OPERATION ABLE—ABLE'S POOL OF
    TEMPORARIES
PAGE BUSINESS SERVICES
PEOPLE INCORPORATED—TEMP SVC
PERSONNEL POOL OF AMERICA
PROFILE TEMPORARY SERVICE INC
READY-MEN INC
STAFF BUILDERS
STIVERS TEMPORARY PERSONNEL
SYSTEMP OF CHICAGO
WHITE COLLAR SERVICES

CHICAGO HEIGHTS
DAVIS TEMPORARIES INC

CRYSTAL LAKE
WORKING WORLD INC

DECATUR
TEMP FORCE OF DECATUR

DEERFIELD
ADIA PERSONNEL SERVICES
STIVERS TEMPORARY PERSONNEL
TEMP/HELP

DES PLAINES
CDI TEMPORARY SERVICES INC
NORRELL SERVICES
STIVERS TEMPORARY PERSONNEL
WHITE COLLAR SERVICES LTD

DOWNERS GROVE
ADIA PERSONNEL SERVICES
GROVE TEMPORARY SERVICES INC

ELK GROVE
UNIFORCE TEMPORARY SERVICES

ELMHURST
ADIA PERSONNEL SERVICES

ELMWOOD PARK
ADIA PERSONNEL SERVICES

EVANSTON
STIVERS TEMPORARY PERSONNEL

FAIRVIEW HEIGHTS
ADIA PERSONNEL SERVICES
TEMP FORCE OF FAIRVIEW HEIGHTS

GLENDALE HEIGHTS
ANN LYNNE TEMPORARIES INC

HAZEL CREST
ADIA PERSONNEL SERVICES

JOLIET
ADIA PERSONNEL SERVICES
GENIE TEMPORARY SERVICES
TEMP/HELP LTD

LA GRANGE
WHITE COLLAR SERVICES

LIBERTYVILLE
ADIA PERSONNEL SERVICES

LINCOLNWOOD
PERSONNEL POOL OF AMERICA

MACOMB
ADIA PERSONNEL SERVICES

MOLINE
TEMP FORCE OF MOLINE

MOUNT PROSPECT
WHITE COLLAR SERVICES

NAPERVILLE
NORRELL SERVICES
PERSONNEL POOL OF AMERICA
TEMP FORCE OF NAPERVILLE
TEMP/HELP LTD

NILES
DEBBIE TEMPS INC

NORTHBROOK
VICTOR TEMPORARY SERVICES

OAK BROOK
NORRELL SERVICES
PERSONNEL POOL OF AMERICA
SALEM SERVICES
STIVERS TEMP PERSONNEL INC
WHITE COLLAR SERVICES

OAK LAWN
ADIA PERSONNEL SERVICES
NORRELL SERVICES

OAK PARK
ADIA PERSONNEL SERVICES

OAKBROOK
STAFF BUILDERS

OAKBROOK TERRACE
ADIA PERSONNEL SERVICES
SALEM SERVICES INC
SNELLING TEMPORARIES
TEM PRO RESOURCES INC

PALATINE
BLAIR BUSINESS SERVICES INC

PARK RIDGE
NATION-WIDE SERVICES INC

PEORIA
NORRELL SERVICES

QUINCY
ADIA PERSONNEL SERVICES

RIVER FOREST
PERSONNEL POOL OF AMERICA

ROCKFORD
EMPLOYMENT RESOURCES INC
FURST TEMPORARY SERVICES
GAFFNEY EMPLOYMENT SVCS INC
NED DICKEY TEMPORARIES
NORRELL SERVICES
SELECTABILITY

SCHAUMBURG
ADIA PERSONNEL SERVICES
NORRELL SERVICES
PERSONNEL POOL OF AMERICA
SNELLING TEMPORARIES
STIVERS TEMPORARY PERSONNEL
TODAYS TEMPORARIES

SKOKIE
ADIA PERSONNEL SERVICES
CLAIMTEMPS INC OF ILLINOIS
NORRELL SERVICES
READY-MEN INC

SPRINGFIELD
EXPRESS SERVICES INC
NORRELL SERVICES

WEST DUNDEE
T.H.E. AGENCY INCORPORATED

WHEELING
DEBBIE TEMPS

INDIANA

ELKHART
PERSONNEL POOL OF AMERICA

EVANSVILLE
NORRELL SERVICES

FARMINGTON HILLS
J MARTIN TEMPS PLUS

FORT WAYNE
ADIA PERSONNEL SERVICES
FLEXIBLE TEMPORARIES
NORRELL SERVICES
PERSONNEL POOL OF AMERICA
TIME SERVICES INC

INDIANAPOLIS
ADIA PERSONNEL SERVICES
CDI TEMPORARY SERVICES INC
CROWN SERVICES
DUNHILL TEMPORARY SYSTEMS
ETC TEMPORARY SERVICES INC
ITT EMPLOYER SERVICES INC
NORRELL SERVICES
OFFICE AID
PERSONNEL POOL OF AMERICA
STANDBY OFFICE SERVICE
TEMP FORCE OF INDIANAPOLIS
TEMPORARIES INCORPORATED
TRC TEMPORARY SERVICES INC

LAFAYETTE
BOYER'S TEMPORARY HELP SERVICE

MERRILLVILLE
TEMP FORCE OF MERRILLVILLE

SHELBYVILLE
PERSONNEL MANAGEMENT INC

SOUTH BEND
NORRELL SERVICES
TEM PRO RESOURCES INC

WARSAW
FLEXIBLE SERVICES INC

IOWA

BETTENDORF
NORRELL SERVICES
TEMPRO SERVICE

CEDAR RAPIDS
NORRELL SERVICES

DES MOINES
NORRELL SERVICES
PERSONNEL POOL OF AMERICA

MUSCATINE
TEMP ASSOCIATES

WEST DES MOINES
CDI TEMPORARY SERVICES INC
STAFF-TEMPS

KANSAS

LEAWOOD
TEMPORARIES INC

OVERLAND PARK
ADIA PERSONNEL SERVICES
CDI TEMPORARY SERVICES INC
PERSONNEL POOL OF AMERICA
SNELLING TEMPORARIES
STAFF BUILDERS

SHAWNEE MISSION
TEMP FORCE OF SHAWNEE MISSION

TOPEKA
DUNHILL TEMPORARY SYSTEMS

WICHITA
DUNHILL TEMPORARY SYSTEMS
NORRELL SERVICES
PERSONNEL POOL OF AMERICA

KENTUCKY

CRESCENT SPRINGS
PERSONNEL POOL OF AMERICA

FLORENCE
ADIA PERSONNEL SERVICES
CROWN SERVICES

FRANKFORT
NORRELL SERVICES

GEORGETOWN
NORRELL SERVICES

LEXINGTON
ADIA PERSONNEL SERVICES
C.M. TEMPORARY SERVICES
JBS INC
NORRELL SERVICES
PERSONNEL POOL OF AMERICA
SNELLING TEMPORARIES
TEMPS EMPLOYMENT INC

LONDON
JOB SHOP EMPLOYMENT
 AGENCY-THE

LOUISVILLE
ADIA PERSONNEL SERVICES
CROWN SERVICES
DATASSISTANTS
METRO TEMPORAIRES INC

NORRELL SERVICES
OLSTEN TEMPORARY SERVICES
PAULA YORK PERSONNEL INC
PERSONNEL POOL OF AMERICA
SWISHER CORPORATION

LOUISIANA

BATON ROUGE
NORRELL SERVICES

GRETNA
NORRELL SERVICES

LAFAYETTE
NORRELL SERVICES

METAIRIE
ADIA PERSONNEL SERVICES
NORRELL SERVICES
PRO-TEM SERVICES INC
VICTOR TEMPORARY SERVICES

NEW ORLEANS
NORRELL SERVICES
STAFF BUILDERS
TALENT TREE TEMPORARIES
TEMP FORCE OF NEW ORLEANS
WORKLOAD TEMPORARY SERVICES

MAINE

PORTLAND
DUNHILL TEMPORARY SYSTEMS OF
 PORTLAND INC
PERSONNEL POOL OF AMERICA

ROCKLAND
ASSOCIATED SERVICES OF ALL KINDS

MARYLAND

ABINGDON
STAFF BUILDERS

ANNAPOLIS
INTERIM PERSONNEL INC

BALTIMORE
ABLE TEMPORARIES
ADIA PERSONNEL SERVICES
ASSURED MEDICAL TEMPS INC
BF&M TEMPS INC
BSI TEMPORARIES INC
CDI TEMPORARY SERVICES INC
COMPUTER RELATED TEMPORARIES
CONTROL DATA TEMPS
NORRELL SERVICES
PERSONNEL POOL OF AMERICA
PROTEMPS INC

SES TEMPS INC
SNELLING TEMPORARIES
STAFF BUILDERS
TELE SEC TEMPORARY SERVICES
TODAYS TEMPORARIES

BETHESDA
NORRELL SERVICES
TEMPORARIES INC

CHEVERLY
TRACY TEMPORARIES INC

COLUMBIA
CDI TEMPORARY SERVICES INC
STAFF BUILDERS

EASTON
PROFESSIONAL TEMPORARIES

FALLSTON
STAFF BUILDERS

FREDERICK
DUNHILL PERSONNEL OF FREDERICK
INC

GAITHERSBURG
ADIA PERSONNEL SERVICES
GOODFRIEND TEMPORARY SERVICES
SPARKS PERSONNEL SERVICES INC
TELE SEC TEMPORARY SERVICES
TEMPORARIES INC

GREENBELT
GOODFRIEND TEMPORARY SERVICES

HANOVER
MEDICAL HOME SERVICES INC

HYATTSVILLE
RAPID WRITER TEMPORARY SVCS
TELE SEC TEMPORARY SERVICES

KENSINGTON
TELE SEC TEMPORARY SERVICES

LANDOVER
ADIA PERSONNEL SERVICES
BSI TEMPORARIES INC
SPARKS PERSONNEL SERVICES INC

LAUREL
BSI TEMPORARIES INC

LUTHERVILLE
NORRELL SERVICES

ROCKVILLE
ADIA PERSONNEL SERVICES
ADVANTAGE INC
DUNHILL TEMPORARY SYSTEMS

GOODFRIEND TEMPORARY SERVICES
INGRID'S TEMPS, DIVISION OF
MONARCH TEMPORARY SVCS (TS)
NORRELL SERVICES
TEMPORARY RESOURCES

SALISBURY
SNELLING TEMPORARIES

SILVER SPRING
BSI TEMPORARIES INC

TIMONIUM
BSI TEMPORARIES INC
SNELLING TEMPORARIES
STAFF BUILDERS

TOWSON
ADIA PERSONNEL SERVICES
MARGE FOX PERSONNEL SERVICES
INC
TEMP FORCE OF TOWSON

WHEATON
GOODFRIEND TEMPORARY SERVICES
SPARKS PERSONNEL SERVICES INC
STAFF BUILDERS

MASSACHUSETTS

ACTON
OFFICE SPECIALISTS

ATTLEBORO
ADIA PERSONNEL SERVICES

BOSTON
ADIA PERSONNEL SERVICES
ARBOR ASSOCIATES
CDI TEMPORARY SERVICES INC
DUNHILL TEMPORARY SYSTEMS
KENNISON, NASSBAUM, FIOL &
TUCKER INC
MEDICAL REGISTER INC
OFFICE SPECIALISTS
PEAKLOAD SERVICES
PERSONNEL POOL OF AMERICA
PREFERRED TEMPORARIES INC
SKILL BUREAU, THE
STAFF BUILDERS
STAT
TAD TECHNICAL SERVICES CORP
TEMPLOYMENT
TEMPORARIES INC
TRACY TEMPORARIES INC
UNIFORCE TEMPORARIES OF BOSTON
VOLT TEMPORARY SERVICES

BRAINTREE
OMNI PERSONNEL SERVICES

BROCKTON
EASTERN STATES INDUSTRIAL
SERVICE INC
OMNI PERSONNEL SERVICES
STAFF BUILDERS

BROOKLINE
OFFICE SPECIALISTS

BURLINGTON
NORRELL SERVICES
OFFICE SPECIALISTS
OXFORD & ASSOCIATES INC
TEMPORARY SOLUTIONS INC

CAMBRIDGE
ADIA PERSONNEL SERVICES
CDI TEMPORARY SERVICES INC
OFFICE SPECIALISTS
TAD TEMPORARIES
VOLT TEMPORARY SERVICES

CHARLESTOWN
TEMPORARIES INC

CHELMSFORD
ADIA PERSONNEL SERVICES
OFFICE SPECIALISTS
VOLT TEMPORARY SERVICES

EDISON
ADIA PERSONNEL SERVICES

FAIRHAVEN
SNELLING TEMPORARIES

FRAMINGHAM
ADIA PERSONNEL SERVICES
JBS INC
NEW ENGLAND TEMPS INC
OFFICE SPECIALISTS

GLOUCESTER
AID TEMPORARY SERVICES

GREENFIELD
HARMON TEMPORARY SERVICE

LAWRENCE
BROOK STREET BUREAU DIV OF
RIVERWALK

LEOMINSTER
APPLESEED PERSONNEL SERVICES

LEXINGTON
ADIA PERSONNEL SERVICES
KLEVEN TEMPS INC

LIVINGSTON
ADIA PERSONNEL SERVICES

LYNN
TEMP FORCE OF LYNN

MALDEN
OFFICE SPECIALISTS
VOLT TEMPORARY SERVICES

MARSTON MILLS
TEMPORARILY YOURS

METHUEN
OFFICE SPECIALISTS

MILLFORD
OFFICE SPECIALISTS

NATICK
STIVERS TEMPORARY PERSONNEL

NEEDHAM
ADIA PERSONNEL SERVICES
CAREER CENTER INC

NEWTON UPPER FALLS
TAC/TEMPS INC

NORTH DARTMOUTH
ADIA PERSONNEL SERVICES

NORWOOD
BUCKINGHAM PERSONNEL SERVICES

PEABODY
OFFICE SPECIALISTS

PLYMOUTH
ALLIED PERSONNEL SERVICES INC

QUINCY
ANODYNE CORPORATION
OFFICE SPECIALISTS
OMNI PERSONNEL SERVICES

READING
OXFORD & ASSOCIATES INC

SALEM
AID TEMPORARY SERVICES
HAWTHORNE NURSING REGISTRY INC

SHREWSBURY
NORRELL SERVICES

SOUTH NATICK
FAITH CASLER ASSOCIATES INC

SPRINGFIELD
DUNHILL TEMPORARY SYSTEMS
UNITED TEMPORARIES OF
    MASSACHUSETTS

STONEHAM
OFFICE SPECIALISTS

STOUGHTON
OFFICE SPECIALISTS

WAKEFIELD
ADIA PERSONNEL SERVICES
OFFICE SPECIALISTS

WALTHAM
ADDITIONAL TECH SUPPORT INC
ADIA PERSONNEL SERVICES
OFFICE SPECIALISTS
SULLIVAN & COGLIANO COMPANIES,
    THE
UNIFORCE TEMPORARY SERVICES

WEST SPRINGFIELD
PERSONNEL POOL OF AMERICA
TEMPOSITIONS

WEYMOUTH
NORRELL SERVICES
OFFICE SPECIALISTS

WINTHROP
OMNIHELP INC

WOBURN
ADIA PERSONNEL SERVICES
AID TEMPORARY SERVICES
SEARCH TEMPS INC
STAFF BUILDERS
VOLT TEMPORARY SERVICES

WORCESTER
APPLESEED PERSONNEL SERVICES
DUNHILL TEMPORARY SYSTEMS
FIRST TEMPORARY SERVICES
PERSONNEL POOL OF AMERICA
STIVERS TEMPORARY PERSONNEL

MICHIGAN

ADRIAN
ADIA PERSONNEL SERVICES

ANN ARBOR
ADIA PERSONNEL SERVICES
ARBOR TEMPORARIES
ASSOCIATED INFORMATION
    CONSULTANTS INC
J. MARTIN TEMPORARIES, PLUS
NORRELL SERVICES
PERSONNEL POOL OF AMERICA
WOLVERINE TEMPORARIES INC

AUBURN HILLS
ADIA PERSONNEL SERVICES
BENCHMARK TEMPORARY SERVICES
ENTECH SERVICES LTD

BATTLE CREEK
EMPLOYMENT SERVICES GROUP
PERSONNEL POOL OF AMERICA

BIRMINGHAM
UNIFORCE TEMPORARY SERVICES

BRIGHTON
ADIA PERSONNEL SERVICES

BROOKLYN
ADIA PERSONNEL SERVICES

BURTON
ADIA PERSONNEL SERVICES

COLDWATER
PERSONNEL POOL OF AMERICA

DEARBORN
ADIA PERSONNEL SERVICES
NORRELL SERVICES

DEARBORN HEIGHTS
PERSONNEL POOL OF AMERICA

DETROIT
ADIA PERSONNEL SERVICES
CDI TEMPORARY SERVICES INC
EMPLOYERS TEMPORARY SERV INC
ENTECH SERVICES LTD
TRC TEMPORARY SERVICES INC

EAST DETROIT
BENCHMARK TEMPORARY SERVICES
PERSONNEL POOL OF AMERICA
WORDS-ON-WHEELS USA

EAST LANSING
TEMP FORCE OF LANSING
UNIFORCE TEMPORARY SERVICES

FARMINGTON HILLS
ADIA PERSONNEL SERVICES
NORRELL SERVICES

FLINT
GREATER FLINT TEMPORARIES LTD
TRIALON CORPORATION

GRAND RAPIDS
ADIA PERSONNEL SERVICES
EMPLOYMENT SERVICES GROUP
J MARTIN TEMPS PLUS
PERSONNEL POOL OF AMERICA
SNELLING TEMPORARIES
TEMP FORCE OF GRAND RAPIDS

HILLSDALE
ADIA PERSONNEL SERVICES

JACKSON
ADIA PERSONNEL SERVICES

KALAMAZOO
ADIA PERSONNEL SERVICES
EMPLOYMENT SERVICES GROUP
PERSONNEL POOL OF AMERICA

LAKE ORION
WORKFORCE INCORPORATED

LANSING
ADIA PERSONNEL SERVICES
EMPLOYMENT SERVICES GROUP
PPL

LATHRUP VILLAGE
STAFF BUILDERS

LIVONIA
ACRO SERVICE CORPORATION
ADIA PERSONNEL SERVICES
BENCHMARK TEMPOARY SERVICES
BENCHMARK TEMPORARY SERVICES
STAFF BUILDERS

MADISON HEIGHTS
AERO DETROIT

MONROE
STAFF BUILDERS

MOUNT PLEASANT
PPI LTD

PLYMOUTH
ARBOR TEMPORARIES
  INC/PERSONNEL SYSTEMS

PONTIAC
PERSONNEL POOL OF AMERICA

ROCHESTER
NORRELL SERVICES

SAINT JOSEPH
BEACON SERVICES
EMPLOYMENT SERVICES GROUP
PROFESSIONAL PERSONNEL LEASING
SCOPE SERVICES INC

SOUTHFIELD
ADIA PERSONNEL SERVICES
CDI TEMPORARY SERVICES INC
DAVIS-SMITH MEDICAL DENTAL
ENTECH SERVICES LTD
PARTNERS IN PLACEMENT
PERSONNEL POOL OF AMERICA
SNELLING TEMPORARIES
TEMPORARY RESOURCES
TROJAN ENGINEERING CO
UNIFORCE TEMPORARY SERVICES

STERLING HEIGHTS
ADIA PERSONNEL SERVICES
CDI TEMPORARY SERVICES INC
TRC TEMPORARY SERVICES INC

STURGIS
PERSONNEL POOL OF AMERICA

TROY
C & T TECHNICAL SERVICES CORP
CDI TEMPORARY SERVICES INC
CONTEMPRA TEMPORARY
  PERSONNEL
ENTECH SERVICES LTD
KELLY SERVICES INC

WARREN
NORRELL SERVICES

WYANDOTTE
ADIA PERSONNEL SERVICES

YPSILANTI
ADIA PERSONNEL SERVICES

MINNESOTA

BLOOMINGTON
ALTERNATIVE STAFFING INC
CDI TEMPORARY SERVICES INC
QUALITY TEMP INC

BROOKLYN CENTER
CDI TEMPORARY SERVICES INC
PERSONNEL POOL OF AMERICA

BURNSVILLE
PERSONNEL PLACEMENTS INC

DULUTH
NORRELL SERVICES

EDINA
ADIA PERSONNEL SERVICES
JEWELL PERSONNEL INC
NORRELL SERVICES
PERSONNEL POOL OF AMERICA

GOLDEN VALLEY
TEMPORARY ASSETS INC

MINNEAPOLIS
ADIA PERSONNEL SERVICES
CONTROL DATA TEMPS
CROWN SERVICES
DOBBS TEMPORARY SERVICES INC
SOLMARK TEMPORARY SERVICES
STAFF BUILDERS
STAFF-PLUS INC
STIVERS TEMPORARY PERSONNEL
TELE-TEMPS

MONTICELLO
ACTION-PLUS TEMPORARY SVC INC

NEW HOPE
EXPRESS SERVICES INC

NORTH MANKATO
EXPRESS SERVICES INC

OWATONNA
EXPRESS SERVICES INC

ROCHESTER
EXPRESS SERVICES INC

ROGERS
TEMPORARY ASSETS INC

SAINT CLOUD
EXPRESS SERVICES INC

SAINT LOUIS PARK
CDI TEMPORARY SERVICES INC

SAINT PAUL
ADIA PERSONNEL SERVICES
FREELANCE PROFESSIONALS INC
JEANE THORNE TEMPORARY
  SERVICES INC
NORRELL SERVICES
PERSONNEL POOL OF AMERICA
STAFF BUILDERS

SANTA FE
ARROW AND AND-EX TEMPORARY
  HELP

SHOREVIEW
NORRELL SERVICES

MISSISSIPPI

JACKSON
JACKSON TEMPORARIES INC
NORRELL SERVICES
TEMP FORCE OF JACKSON-
  MISSISSIPPI

OLIVE BRANCH
NORRELL SERVICES

MISSOURI

AFFTON
ADIA PERSONNEL SERVICES

CAMDENTON
JEANNE'S PROFESSIONAL SERVICES
  INC

CHESTERFIELD
ADIA PERSONNEL SERVICES
B. LOEHR TEMPORARIES
CDI TEMPORARY SERVICES INC

CLAYTON
ADIA PERSONNEL SERVICES
CDI TEMPORARY SERVICES INC
DUNHILL TEMPORARY SYSTEMS
SNELLING TEMPORARIES

CREVE COEUR
ADIA PERSONNEL SERVICES
SNELLING TEMPORARIES

GLADSTONE
ADIA PERSONNEL SERVICES
PERSONNEL POOL OF AMERICA

HANNIBAL
ADIA PERSONNEL SERVICES

KANSAS CITY
ADIA PERSONNEL SERVICES
CDI TEMPORARY SERVICES INC
CROWN SERVICES
DUNHILL TEMPORARY SYSTEMS
EXPRESS SERVICES INC
NORRELL SERVICES
PERSONNEL POOL OF AMERICA
STIVERS TEMPORARY PERSONNEL
TRC TEMPORARY SERVICES INC
UNIFORCE TEMPORARY SERVICES

MARYLAND HEIGHTS
CDI TEMPORARY SERVICES INC

NORTH KANSAS CITY
EXPRESS SERVICES INC

ROLLA
EXPRESS SERVICES INC

SAINT ANN
B. LOEHR TEMPORARIES
STIVERS TEMPORARY PERSONNEL

SAINT JOSEPH
EXPRESS SERVICES INC

SAINT LOUIS
ADIA PERSONNEL SERVICES
B. LOEHR TEMPORARIES
CDI TEMPORARY SERVICES INC
CROWN SERVICES
JBS INC
NORRELL SERVICES
PERSONNEL POOL OF AMERICA
STAFF BUILDERS
TEMP FORCE-ST. LOUIS MISSOURI
TODAYS TEMPORARIES
TRC TEMPORARY SERVICES INC

SPRINGFIELD
PERSONNEL POOL OF AMERICA

MONTANA

BILLINGS
ARROW AND AND-EX TEMPORARY
  HELP
EXPRESS SERVICES INC
TEMPORARY CONNECTION, THE

BOZEMAN
ARROW AND AND-EX TEMPORARY
  HELP
EXPRESS SERVICES INC

BUTTE
EXPRESS SERVICES INC

GREAT FALLS
ARROW AND AND-EX TEMPORARY
  HELP
EXPRESS SERVICES INC

HELENA
EXPRESS SERVICES INC
TEMPORARY AND AND-EX
  TEMPORARY HELP

KALISPELL
ARROW AND AND-EX TEMPORARY
  HELP
EXPRESS SERVICES INC
FLATHEAD VALLEY LABOR
  CONTRACTORS INC

MISSOULA
ARROW & AND-EX TEMPORARY HELP
  INC
EXPRESS SERVICES INC

NEBRASKA

LINCOLN
EXPRESS SERVICES INC
NORRELL SERVICES
TEMP FORCE OF LINCOLN
TODAYS TEMPORARIES

OMAHA
CDI TEMPORARY SERVICES INC
CROWN SERVICES
HELP INC
INC SERVICES INC—TEMPORARY
  PERSONNEL
NORRELL SERVICES
PERSONNEL POOL OF AMERICA
SNELLING TEMPORARIES

NEVADA

LAS VEGAS
ADIA PERSONNEL SERVICES
MEDI-GIRLS INC
STAFF BUILDERS

RENO
TEMP FORCE OF RENO
TRANSWORLD TEMPORARIES

SPARKS
PERSONNEL SERVICES INC

NEW HAMPSHIRE

GREENLAND
UNIFORCE TEMPORARY SERVICES

KEENE
TRI-STATE PROFESSIONALS INC

MANCHESTER
OFFICE SPECIALISTS
PERSONNEL POOL OF AMERICA

NASHUA
NORRELL SERVICES
OFFICE SPECIALISTS
OXFORD & ASSOCIATES INC
PREFERRED POSITIONS INC
WORK FORCE INC

NORTH HAMPTON
KEY PERSONNEL

WEST LEBANON
TEMPORARY CONNECTION, THE

NEW JERSEY

ATLANTIC CITY
JOULE TEMPORARIES

BELLE MEAD
PROFESSIONAL TEMPS INC

BERLIN
TEMP SOURCE INC, THE

BLOOMFIELD
AUBREY THOMAS TEMPORARIES

CHATHAM
STAFF BUILDERS

CHERRY HILL
ACCU TEMPORARY SERVICES
COMPUTER RELATED TEMPORARIES
  (CRT)
DUNHILL TEMPORARY SYSTEMS
JOULE TEMPORARIES
STAFF BUILDERS

CLIFTON
STAFF BUILDERS

CRANFORD
STAFF BUILDERS

EAST BRUNSWICK
CDI TEMPORARY SERVICES INC
SNELLING TEMPORARIES
TODAYS TEMPORARIES

EATONTOWN
CDI TEMPORARY SERVICES INC
JOULE TEMPORARIES
SNELLING TEMPORARIES

EDISON
CITTONE TEMPS
DUNHILL PERSONNEL OF MIDDLESEX
JONATHAN ROYCE INTERNATIONAL
JOULE TEMPORARIES
SYSTEMP
TODAYS TEMPORARIES
TRANSWORLD TEMPORARIES

ELIZABETH
G-P TEMPS

FAR HILLS
JEAN BASSETT AGENCY INC

FREEHOLD
OMNI TEMPS INC
SAMEDAY TEMPS
TRANSWORLD TEMPORARIES

HACKENSACK
COMPUTER RELATED TEMPORARIES
KEYES TEMPS
PERSONNEL POOL OF AMERICA

HAMILTON SQUARE
TRANSWORLD TEMPORARIES

HIGHLAND PARK
COSMOPOLITAN CARE CORPORATION

HOLMDEL
ADIA PERSONNEL SERVICES

IRVINGTON
STAFF BUILDERS

JAMESBURG
NORRELL SERVICES

JERSEY CITY
READY TEMPS INC

LAKE HIAWATH
STAFF BUILDERS

LAWRENCEVILLE
CDI TEMPORARY SERVICES INC
NORRELL SERVICES

MAHWAH
UNITEMP TEMPORARY PERSONNEL

MARLTON
ADIA PERSONNEL SERVICES
CDI TEMPORARY SERVICES INC

MONTVALE
JOULE TEMPORARIES

MORRISTOWN
AUBREY THOMAS TEMPORARIES
COSMOPOLITAN CARE CORPORATION
INTERFACE TEMPORARY SERVICES
UNITEMP TEMPORARY PERSONNEL

MOUNT LAUREL
STAFF BUILDERS

NEW BRUNSWICK
STAFF BUILDERS

NORTH BRUNSWICK
ACTION TEMPS INC

PARAMUS
ADIA PERSONNEL SERVICES
AUBREY THOMAS TEMPORARIES
COSMOPOLITAN CARE CORPORATION
JOULE TEMPORARIES
TODAYS TEMPORARIES
UNIFORCE TEMPORARY SERVICES
UNITEMP TEMPORARY PERSONNEL

PARSIPPANY
NEW CAREER PERSONNEL SERVICES
NORRELL SERVICES
PRIME TIME PERSONNEL INC

PATERSON
JBS INC
PERSONNEL POOL OF AMERICA

PENNSAUKEN
NORRELL SERVICES

PISCATAWAY
ADIA PERSONNEL SERVICES
DIAL A TEMPORARY

PLAINSBORO
ADIA PERSONNEL SERVICES
COSMOPOLITAN CARE CORPORATION

POINT PLEASANT BEACH
ADIA PERSONNEL SERVICES

PRINCETON
DUNHILL TEMPORARY SYSTEMS
STAFF BUILDERS

ROCHELLE PARK
STAFF BUILDERS

RUTHERFORD
UNIFORCE TEMPORARY SERVICES

SCOTCH PLAINS
APOXIFORCE, A-1 IN TEMPORARIES

SECAUCUS
JOULE TEMPORARIES
SYSTEMP
UNITEMP TEMPORARY PERSONNEL

SHREWSBURY
ADIA PERSONNEL SERVICES
NORRELL SERVICES

SOMERSET
PERSONNEL POOL OF AMERICA

SUMMIT
UNIFORCE TEMPORARY SERVICES

TOM'S RIVER
ADIA PERSONNEL SERVICES

TRENTON
JOULE TEMPORARIES

UNION
AUBREY THOMAS TEMPORARIES
JONATHAN ROYCE INTERNATIONAL
JOULE TEMPORARIES

VOORHEES
NORRELL SERVICES

WAYNE
PERSONNEL POOL OF AMERICA
TRANSWORLD TEMPORARIES

WEST ORANGE
NORRELL SERVICES

WHIPPANY
DIAL A TEMPORARY

WOODCLIFF LAKE
UNITEMP TEMPORARY PERSONNEL

NEW MEXICO

ALBUQUERQUE
ADIA PERSONNEL SERVICES
ARROW AND AND-EX TEMPORARY
  HELP
DUNHILL TEMPORARY SYSTEMS
EXPRESS SERVICES INC

NORRELL SERVICES
PERSONNEL POOL OF AMERICA
SNELLING TEMPORARIES
TEMP FORCE OF ALBUQUERQUE
VOLT TEMPORARY SERVICES

FARMINGTON
UNIFORCE/EMPLOY-MINT

HOBBS
EXPRESS SERVICES INC

LAS CRUCES
TEMP FORCE OF LAS CRUCES

ROSWELL
TEMP FORCE OF ROSWELL

SANTA FE
SANTA FE SERVICES INC
SNELLING TEMPORARIES

NEW YORK

ALBANY
NORRELL SERVICES
STAFF BUILDERS
TEMP FORCE OF ALBANY
UNIFORCE OF ALBANY

BINGHAMTON
NORRELL SERVICES

BROOKLYN
TEMP FORCE OF BROOKLYN

BUFFALO
ABLEST SERVICE CORPORATION
CDI TEMPORARY SERVICES INC
COMPUTERPEOPLE
DUNHILL TEMPORARY SYSTEMS
DURHAM TEMPORARIES INC
PERSONNEL POOL OF AMERICA
TEMP CAREERS INC
TEMP FORCE OF BUFFALO

CAMBRIA HEIGHTS
TEMP FORCE/QUEENS

CARLE
DUNHILL TEMPORARY SYSTEMS

CORNING
TEMP FORCE OF CORNING

DEPEW
DURHAM TEMPORARIES INC

EAST MEADOW
COSMOPOLITAN PERSONNEL
  SYSTEMS
WINSTON TEMPORARIES

EAST NORTHPORT
DUNHILL TEMPORARY SYSTEMS

ELMHURST
COSMOPOLITAN CARE CORPORATION
STAFF BUILDERS

FAIRPORT
ADIA PERSONNEL SERVICES

FLUSHING
NYATS

FOREST HILLS
ADIA PERSONNEL SERVICES

GARDEN CITY
STAFF BUILDERS

GLENS FALLS
C.V. KEENA ASSOCIATES

GOSHEN
DAY-OUT TEMPORARY EMPLOYMENT
  SERVICES

HARTSDALE
AUBREY THOMAS TEMPORARIES

HAUPPAUGE
DUNHILL TEMPORARY SYSTEMS

HICKSVILLE
UNIFORCE TEMPORARY SERVICES

JAMAICA
NATIONAL TEMPORARY HELP SERV

JERICHO
ADIA PERSONNEL SERVICES
OFFICE FORCE

JOHNSON CITY
TEMP FORCE OF JOHNSON CITY

LAKE SUCCESS
STAFF BUILDERS

LEVITTOWN
PERSONNEL POOL OF AMERICA

LIVERPOOL
NORRELL SERVICES
PERSONNEL POOL OF AMERICA

LONG ISLAND
AUBREY THOMAS TEMPORARIES

MANHATTAN
STAFF BUILDERS

MELVILLE
CAREER BLAZERS PERSONNEL SVCS
GLOBALFORCE TEMP PERSN
  COMPANY
PERSONNEL POOL OF AMERICA
TEMPOSITIONS INC
UNIFORCE TEMPORARY SERVICES
WINSTON TEMPORARIES

MIDDLETOWN
CAREER DIRECTIONS INC
HERE'S HELP INC

MINEOLA
SNELLING TEMPORARIES

NANUET
HERTZ TEMPORARY SERVICES

NEW CITY
AUBREY THOMAS TEMPORARIES

NEW HYDE PARK
UNIFORCE TEMPORARY SERVICE

NEW ROCHELLE
TEMP FORCE OF WESTCHESTER

NEW YORK
ACCOUNTANCY PERSONNEL INC
ACCOUNTANTS & AUDITORS
  TEMPORARIES
ADIA PERSONNEL SERVICES
ADVANTAGE INC
ASSOCIATED TEMPORARY STAFFING
  INC
AUBREY THOMAS TEMPORARIES
BENEFICIAL TEMPORARIES
BON TEMPS
BROOK ST BUREAU INC
CAREER BLAZERS TEMPORARY
  PERSONNEL
COSMOPOLITAN CARE CORPORATION
CROSS TEMPS INC
EDEN TEMPORARY SERVICES INC
F.L.A.G. SERVICES INC
FORUM TEMP SERVICES
GOSSAGE REGAN ASSOCIATES INC
HOLIDAY TEMPORARY SERVICES INC
HOSPITAL TEMPORARIES
HOURLY HELPERS
INTERIM SYSTEMS INC
IRENE COHEN TEMPS INC
LANDMARK TEMPORARIES INC
LAWRENCE INDUSTRIAL TEMPS
LAWRENCE TEMPORARIES
LEGAL ASSISTANTS CORP
LEGAL RESOURCES/WORDTEMPS
NORRELL SERVICES
OFFICE FORCE

PAYSON PEOPLE INC
PERSONNEL POOL OF AMERICA
PLANNED STAFFING INC
PRO-TEMPS INCORPORATED
SLOAN TEMPORARY SERVICE INC
STAFF BUILDERS INC
SYSTEMP
TECHLANCERS TEMPORARIES INC
TELE-TEMPS INC
TEMP FORCE INC
TEMP FORCE OF WALL STREET
TEMPORARIES INC
TEMPORARILY YOURS PERSONNEL
    SERVICE INC
TEMPOSITIONS INC
TIGER TEMPS INC
UNIFORCE TEMPORARY SERVICES
VOLT INFORMATION SCIENCES INC
WINSTON TEMPORARIES INC

NEWBURGH
CAREER DIRECTIONS INC

NIAGARA FALLS
DURHAM TEMPORARIES INC

OSSINING
CRICKETT PERSONNEL SVC INC

PARSIPPANY
JOULE TEMPORARIES

POUGHKEEPSIE
DUTCHESS TEMPS
NORMAN TEMPORARY SERVICES
TEMP FORCE OF POUGHKEEPSIE

ROCHESTER
ABLEST SERVICE CORPORATION
ADIA PERSONNEL SERVICES
CDI TEMPORARY SERVICES INC
EAGLE TEMPORARY SERVICE INC
EMPLOYMENT STORE INC
EXTRA HELP EMPLOYEE SERVICES
NORRELL SERVICES
PERSONNEL POOL OF AMERICA
SNELLING TEMPORARIES
TAD TECHNICAL SERVICES CORP
TEMP FORCE OF ROCHESTER

SMITHTOWN
A.S.A.P. TEMPORARIES
UNIFORCE TEMPORARY SERVICES

STATEN ISLAND
GERRI G INC

SYRACUSE
ABLEST SERVICES CORPORATION
ADIA PERSONNEL SERVICES
CDI TEMPORARY SERVICES INC
ERNESTWELL LTD
NORRELL SERVICES

PERSONNEL POOL OF AMERICA
TAD TECHNICAL SERVICES CORP

TONAWANDA
DURHAM TEMPORARIES INC

UNIONDALE
GLOBALFORCE TEMP PERSN
    COMPANY

UTICA
TEMP FORCE OF UTICA

WESTBURY
OLSTEN CORPORATION, THE
TEMP FORCE INC

WHITE PLAINS
AUBREY THOMAS TEMPORARIES
CAREER BLAZERS OF WHITE PLAINS
COSMOPOLITAN CARE CORPORATION
DUNHILL TEMPORARY SYSTEMS
PERSONNEL POOL OF AMERICA
SNELLING TEMPORARIES
SYSTEMP
TEMPORARIES INC

WILLIAMSVILLE
DURHAM TEMPORARIES INC
NORRELL SERVICES
VESTAFF INC

NORTH CAROLINA

ASHEVILLE
ADIA PERSONNEL SERVICES
UNIFORCE TEMPORARY SERVICES

BURLINGTON
BLETHEN TEMPORARIES
DUNHILL TEMPORARY SYSTEMS

CARY
OFFICE SPECIALISTS

CHAPEL HILL
MONARCH TEMPORARY SERVICES

CHARLOTTE
ADIA PERSONNEL SERVICES
ASSOCIATED TEMP STAFFING INC
CDI TEMPORARY SERVICES INC
CORPORATE PERSONNEL
    CONSULTANTS & TEMPORARIES INC
CREATIVE TEMPORARIES CORP
DUNHILL TEMPORARY SYSTEMS
NORRELL SERVICES
PERSONNEL POOL OF AMERICA
PHILLIPS STAFFING
RESOURCES EMPLOYMENT SERVICES
TEAM SERVICES INC

TEMPORARIES INC
TEMPWORLD INC
TODAYS TEMPORARIES
TRACY TEMPORARIES INC
UNIFORCE OF CHARLOTTE

CLAYTON
KING TEMPORARY SERVICES

DURHAM
ELITE PERSONNEL SERVICES INC
MONARCH TEMPORARY SERVICES
PERSONNEL POOL OF AMERICA
TEMPORARILY YOURS

FAYETTEVILLE
MEGA FORCE TEMPORARIES
UNIFORCE TEMPORARY SERVICES

GASTONIA
DUNHILL TEMPORARY SYSTEMS
UNIFORCE TEMPORARY SERVICES

GREENSBORO
ABLEST SERVICES CORPORATION
ADIA PERSONNEL SERVICES
B & B PERSONNEL SERVICE INC
BECKS TEMPORARY SERVICES INC
DUNHILL TEMPORARY SYSTEMS
GRAHAM & ASSOC TEMPORARIES INC
NORRELL SERVICES
PERSONNEL POOL OF AMERICA
POPI TEMPORARY SERVICES
TRC TEMPORARY SERVICES INC
UNIFORCE TEMPORARY SERVICES

GREENVILLE
ANNE'S TEMPORARIES INC

HENDERSONVILLE
FRIDAY TEMPORARY SERVICES

HICKORY
DUNHILL TEMPORARY SYSTEMS
UNIFORCE TEMPORARY SERVICES

HIGH POINT
MARLETTE BAKER TEMPORARIES INC
TRIAD TEMPORARY SERVICES INC

JULIAN
MEGA FORCE TEMPORARIES

KINSTON
ANNE'S TEMPORARIES INC
MCCAIN TEMPORARY SERVICES

LAURINBURG
MEGA FORCE TEMPORARIES

LENOIR
DUNHILL TEMPORARY SYSTEMS

LINCOLNTON
DUNHILL TEMPORARY SYSTEMS

MEBANE
MEBANE TEMPORARY SERVICES

MONROE
TPS INC

MORGANTON
HELPING HANDS TEMPORARY SVC

MORRISVILLE
CDI TEMPORARY SERVICES INC

NEW BERN
ANNE'S TEMPORARIES INC

NORTH CHARLOTTE
CDI TEMPORARY SERVICES INC

OXFORD
MONARCH TEMPORARY SERVICES
TEMPORARILY YOURS

RALEIGH
ABLEST SERVICES CORPORATION
CDI TEMPORARY SERVICES INC
MONARCH TEMPORARY SERVICES
NORRELL SERVICES
OFFICE SPECIALISTS
PERSONNEL POOL OF AMERICA
TEMPORARILY YOURS

RALEIGH-DURHAM
ADIA PERSONNEL SERVICES

ROCKY MOUNT
ANNE'S TEMPORARIES INC

SALISBARY
UNIFORCE TEMPORARY SERVICES

SANFORD
UNIFORCE TEMPORARY SERVICES

SHELBY
DUNHILL TEMPORARY SYSTEMS
PERSONNEL SERVICES UNLIMITED

SMITHFIELD
TAYLOR TEMPORARY SERVICES

WASHINGTON
ANNE'S TEMPORARIES INC

WILMINGTON
NORRELL SERVICES

WINSTON-SALEM
CDI TEMPORARY SERVICES INC
EMPLOYERS' RELIEF INC
NORRELL SERVICES
POPI TEMPORARY SERVICES
TODAYS TEMPORARIES
UNIFORCE TEMPORARY SERVICES

OHIO

AKRON
FLEX-TEAM PROFESSIONAL
   TEMPORARIES INC
STAFF BUILDERS
TIMBLIN TEMPORARIES INC

BATH
ACCOUNTING ASSISTANTS

BEACHWOOD
ADIA PERSONNEL SERVICES
EGAR EMPLOYMENT INC
HOURS INC NATIONAL
LEADER PERSONNEL INC
SNELLING TEMPORARIES

BROADWAY HEIGHTS
OHIO TEMPORARY SERVICES

CINCINNATI
ADIA PERSONNEL SERVICES
ADOW PERSONNEL SERVICES OF
   CINCINNATI
CBS TEMPORARY SERVICES INC
CROWN SERVICES
GPA TEMPS
LE GALS OF CINCINNATI
PERSONNEL POOL OF AMERICA
STAFF BUILDERS
TIME SERVICES INC
TRC TEMPORARY SERVICES INC
XLC SERVICES TEMPORARIES &
   PARATECHNICALS

CLEVELAND
ADIA PERSONNEL SERVICES
AREA TEMPS
CDI TEMPORARY SERVICES INC
CROWN SERVICES
FLEX-FORCE EMPLOYMENT SERVICES
FLEX-TEMP EMPLOYMENT SERVICE
LE-GALS INC
NORRELL SERVICES
ROGELL TEMPS
SNELLING TEMPORARIES
STAFF BUILDERS
TIME SERVICES INC

COLUMBUS
ACT-1 TEMPORARIES INC
ADIA PERSONNEL SERVICES
CDI TEMPORARY SERVICES INC
CROWN SERVICES

FLEX-TEMP EMPLOYMENT SERVICE
HOURS INC
NORRELL SERVICES
OMEGA TEMPORARIES INC
PERSONNEL POOL OF AMERICA
PHARMACY PEOPLE
STAFF BUILDERS
TIME SERVICES INC

COSHOCTON
SHANNON TEMPORARY SERVICES INC

DAYTON
CBS TEMPORARY SERVICES
EXTRAHELP TEMPORARY SERVICES
NORRELL SERVICES
PERSONNEL POOL OF AMERICA
PREFERRED TEMPORARY SERVICES
SNELLING TEMPORARIES
STAFF BUILDERS

DEFIANCE
PERSONNEL POOL OF AMERICA

DELAWARE
ADIA PERSONNEL SERVICES

DUBLIN
ADIA PERSONNEL SERVICES
PHARMACY PEOPLE

FINDLAY
ADIA PERSONNEL SERVICES
PERSONNEL POOL OF AMERICA

HAMILTON
PERSONNEL POOL OF AMERICA

INDEPENDENCE
AMERICAN PROFESSIONAL
   TEMPORARIES INC

LAKEWOOD
TARGET TEMPORARIES INC

LANCASTER
INTERIM TEMPORARIES INC

LIMA
NORRELL SERVICES
PERSONNEL POOL OF AMERICA

MANSFIELD
TEMP FORCE OF MANSFIELD

MARYVILLE
ADIA PERSONNEL SERVICES

MENTOR
CROWN SERVICES
STAFF BUILDERS

MIDDLEBURG HIEGHT
CDI TEMPORARY SERVICES INC

MIDDLETOWN
PALMER TEMPS

MILFORD
PJC TEMPS & SERVICES INC

NEWARK
NORRELL SERVICES

PARMA HEIGHTS
STAFF BUILDERS

PERRYSBURG
NORRELL SERVICES
RENHILL TEMPORARIES

PIQUA
BROWNLEE PERSONNEL SVCS INC

ROCKY RIVER
NORRELL SERVICES
OFFICE RESERVES GROUP

SANDUSKY
FLEX-TEMP EMPLOYMENT SVCS INC

SIDNEY
ADIA PERSONNEL SERVICES

SPRINGFIELD
NORRELL SERVICES

SYLVANIA
TEMPORARY STAFFING INC

TOLEDO
ADIA PERSONNEL SERVICES
AIM TEMPORARIES
FLEX-TEMP EMPLOYMENT SERVICES
NORRELL SERVICES
SNELLING TEMPORARIES
STAFF BUILDERS

TROY
STAFF BUILDERS

WEST CHESTER
QUALITY ASSOCIATES INC

WESTLAKE
CDI TEMPORARY SERVICES INC

WOODMERE VILLAGE
CDI TEMPORARY SERVICES INC

WORTHINGTON
CDI TEMPORARY SERVICES INC
SNELLING TEMPORARIES

OKLAHOMA

LAWTON
EXPRESS SERVICES INC

MIDWEST CITY
GENIE GIRLS
GENIE PERSONNEL SERVICES INC

MUSKOGEE
EXPRESS SERVICES INC

OKLAHOMA CITY
ADIA PERSONNEL SERVICES
ALTERNATIVE STAFFING INC
AVANTE LTD
EXPRESS SERVICES INC
GENIE GIRLS
NORRELL SERVICES
PRO-TEMPORARIES
SOONER TEMPORARY SERVICE
TEMP FORCE OF OKLAHOMA CITY
TEMPO INTERNATIONAL
TODAYS TEMPORARIES
TRC TEMPORARY SERVICES INC

SHAWNEE
EXPRESS SERVICES INC

STILLWATER
EXPRESS SERVICES INC

TULSA
ADIA PERSONNEL SERVICES
DUNHILL TEMPORARY SYSTEMS
EXPRESS SERVICES INC
FORD TEMPORARIES
KEY TEMPORARY PERSONNEL INC
NORRELL SERVICES
TEMP FORCE OF TULSA
TOP TEMPORARIES

OREGON

ALBANY
OREGON TEMPORARY SERVICES INC

BEAVERTON
CASCADE TEMPORARY STAFFING
PERSONNEL POOL OF AMERICA
VOLT TEMPORARY SERVICES

BEND
EXPRESS PERSONNEL SERVICE OF
CENTRAL ORG PLACEMENT
AGENCY

CLACKAMAS
OREGON TEMPORARY SERVICES INC

EUGENE
DIVINE-WILLAMETTE INC
EXPRESS SERVICES INC
OREGON TEMPORARY SERVICES INC
SELECTEMP CORPORATION

MCMINNVILLE
QUALITY PLUS TEMPORARY
EMPLOYEES

MEDFORD
EXPRESS SERVICES INC

PENDLETON
EXPRESS SERVICES INC

PORTLAND
ADIA PERSONNEL SERVICES
DUNHILL TEMPORARY SYSTEMS OF
PORTLAND
EXPRESS SERVICES INC
STAFF BUILDERS
VOLT TEMPORARY SERVICES

ROSEBURG
EXPRESS SERVICES INC

PENNSYLVANIA

ALLENTOWN
ADIA PERSONNEL SERVICES
ALLIED TEMPORARY SERVICES
CDI TEMPORARY SERVICES INC
HCSC MEDICAL PLACEMENT SVCS
NORRELL SERVICES
PERSONNEL POOL OF AMERICA
RUSSOLI TEMPS
TRANSWORLD TEMPORARIES
UNIFORCE TEMPORARY SERVICES

BALA CYNWYD
ADIA PERSONNEL SERVICES
LIZ FRANK PERSONNEL SVC INC
NORRELL SERVICES
STAFF BUILDERS
T/A LONDON TEMPS

BLUE BELL
CDI TEMPORARY SERVICES INC
VALLEYSTAFF INCORPORATED

CARLISLE
ADIA PERSONNEL SERVICES

CARNEGIE
TEMP FORCE OF PITTSBURGH

CHAMBERSBURG
ADIA PERSONNEL SERVICES

EASTON
ADIA PERSONNEL SERVICES

ERIE
JACK B LARSEN & ASSOCIATES

EXTON
ADIA PERSONNEL SERVICES

FEASTERVILLE
ADIA PERSONNEL SERVICES
AMERICAN TEMP SERVICES INC
DUNHILL TEMPORARY SYSTEMS
TEMP FORCE OF BUCKS COUNTY

FORT WASHINGTON
NORRELL SERVICES

FRANKLIN CENTER
NORRELL SERVICES

GREENTREE WEST
ADIA PERSONNEL SERVICES

HANOVER
ADIA PERSONNEL SERVICES
NORRELL SERVICES

HARRISBURG
ADIA PERSONNEL SERVICES
PERSONNEL POOL OF AMERICA

HORSHAM
ADIA PERSONNEL SERVICES
CDI TEMPORARY SERVICES INC

IRWIN
TEMP SERVICES

KING OF PRUSSIA
ADIA PERSONNEL SERVICES
AUBREY THOMAS TEMPORARIES
CDI TEMPORARY SERVICES INC
COMPUTER RELATED TEMPORARIES
NORRELL SERVICES
WORK FORCE INC
WORK FORCE TEMPORARY HELP SVC

KINGSTON
PERSONNEL POOL OF AMERICA

LANCASTER
ADIA PERSONNEL SERVICES
BYRNES GROUP, THE
CDI TEMPORARY SERVICES INC
COMPUTER ADVISORY GROUP
NORRELL SERVICES
PERSONNEL POOL OF AMERICA
TEMPORARY RESOURCES
UNIFORCE TEMPORARY SERVICES

LATROBE
PRS CONSULTANTS

LEBANON
TEMP FORCE OF LEBANON

LEMOYNE
CAPITAL AREA TEMPORARY SERVICE
NORRELL SERVICES
TEMP FORCE OF HARRISBURG

MALVERN
CDI TEMPORARY SERVICES INC

MEADOW LANDS
PROFESSIONALLY YOURS,
  TEMPORARY SERVICES

MECHANICSBURG
BYRNES GROUP, THE
UNITED TEMPS

MEDIA
CDI TEMPORARY SERVICES INC
EAGLE STAFFERS & PLACERS
NORRELL SERVICES
PYRAMID TEMPORARY SERVICES INC
WORK FORCE INC
WORK FORCE TEMPORARY HELP SVC

MONROEVILLE
ADIA PERSONNEL SERVICES
ALZED ENTERPRISES LTD
CAROL HARRIS TEMPORARIES

PHILADELPHIA
ADIA PERSONNEL SERVICES
AUBREY THOMAS TEMPORARIES
CDI TEMPORARY SERVICES INC
COMPUTER RELATED TEMPORARIES
E J BETTINGER COMPANY
KIEFER SERVICES INC
NORRELL SERVICES
PERSONNEL POOL OF AMERICA
SNELLING TEMPORARIES
STAFF BUILDERS
STANDBY TEMPORARY SERVICES
STIVERS TEMPORARY PERSONNEL
SYSTEMP

PITTSBURGH
ADIA PERSONNEL SERVICES
ADMIRAL TEMP SERVICE INC
ALLEGHENY PERSONNEL SERVICES
ALLSTAFF TEMPORARY SERVICES
ALZED ENTERPRISES LTD
CROWN SERVICES
LEGAL MANAGEMENT SERVICES INC
MARSETTA LANE TEMP-SERVICE INC
PANCOAST TEMPORARY SVCS INC
PERSONNEL POOL OF AMERICA
REFLEX SERVICES INC
SNELLING TEMPORARIES

STAFF BUILDERS
TEMPORARIES INC
TIME SERVICES INC

QUAKERTOWN
RUSSOLI TEMPS
STAFF BUILDERS

READING
GAGE-HANDY PERSONNEL SERVICES
PEOPLE UNLIMITED INC
PERSONNEL POOL OF AMERICA

SCRANTON
CDI TEMPORARY SERVICES INC
NORRELL SERVICES
PERSONNEL POOL OF AMERICA
UNIFORCE TEMPORARY SERVICES

STROUDSBURG
RUSSOLI TEMPS

SWATHMORE
ETC OFFICE SYSTEMS SERVICE

VILLANOVA
EAGLE STAFFERS & PLACERS

WAYNE
BRADLEY TEMPORARIES INC
METRO TEMPS
SNELLING TEMPORARIES
STAFF BUILDERS TEMP PERSONNEL
STIVERS TEMPORARY PERSONNEL

WEST CHESTER
NORRELL SERVICES
WORK FORCE INC

WILKES-BARRE
UNIFORCE TEMPORARY SERVICES

WILLIAMSPORT
DE PASQUALE TEMPS
HATS-HOWE ABOUT TEMPS

WILLOW GROVE
COMPUTER RELATED TEMPORARIES

WYOMISSING
GWR PERSONNEL RESOURCES INC

YORK
ADIA PERSONNEL SERVICES
BYRNES GROUP, THE
EMPLOYMENT EAST TEMPS
NORRELL SERVICES
PERSONNEL POOL OF AMERICA
UNITED TEMPS

PUERTO RICO

GUAYNABO
ADVANCE TEMPORARY SERVICE

HATO REY
PERSONNEL POOL OF AMERICA
SNELLING TEMPORARIES

MAYAGUES
DUNHILL TEMPORARY SYSTEMS

RHODE ISLAND

LEXINGTON
ADIA PERSONNEL SERVICES

LINCOLN
TODAYS TEMPORARIES

PROVIDENCE
ADIA PERSONNEL SERVICES
EMPLOYMENT USA INC
NORRELL SERVICES
OFFICE SPECIALISTS
PERSONNEL POOL OF AMERICA
SERVICES RENDERED INC
STAFF BUILDERS

WARWICK
TODAYS TEMPORARIES

WOONSOCKET
MEDICAL TEMP IMAGES INC

SOUTH CAROLINA

AIKEN
BUSINESS FORCE INC
MR/MS TEMPS
TRC TEMPORARY SERVICES INC

ANDERSON
BUSINESS FORCE INC

CHARLESTON
ADIA PERSONNEL SERVICES
EXEC-AIDS
TEMPO INC

COLUMBIA
BUSINESS FORCE INC
CDI TEMPORARY SERVICES INC
DUNHILL TEMPORARY SYSTEMS
NATIONWIDE SPECIALIZED
  TEMPORARIES
NORRELL SERVICES
PERSONNEL POOL OF AMERICA
UNIFORCE TEMPORARY SERVICES

GREENVILLE
CDI TEMPORARY SERVICES INC
DUNHILL TEMPORARY SYSTEMS
NORRELL SERVICES
PEOPLE BUSINESS, THE

PERSONNEL POOL OF AMERICA
PHILLIPS STAFFING SERVICES
SNELLING TEMPORARIES
TEAM SERVICES INC

HILTON HEAD
TEMPO PERSONNEL SERVICES INC

LANCASTER
DUNHILL TEMPORARY SYSTEMS
UNIFORCE TEMPORARY SERVICES

MYRTLE BEACH
BUSINESS FORCE INC

NORTH CHARLESTON
ABACUS TEMPORARY SERVICES
NORRELL SERVICES
PERSONNEL POOL OF AMERICA

ORANGEBURG
BUSINESS FORCE INC

ROCK HILL
CDI TEMPORARY SERVICES INC
DUNHILL TEMPORARY SYSTEMS
PHILLIPS STAFFING SERVICES
UNIFORCE TEMPORARY SERVICES

SPARTANBURG
PHILLIPS STAFFING SERVICES

SOUTH DAKOTA

ABERDEEN
EXPRESS SERVICES INC

RAPID CITY
EXPRESS SERVICES INC

SIOUX FALLS
STAFF PROS

TENNESSEE

ATHENS
PREFERRED TEMPORARY SERVICES

BRENTWOOD
CDI TEMPORARY SERVICES INC
JANE JONES ENTERPRISES

CHATTANOOGA
NORRELL SERVICES
TEMP FORCE OF CHATTANOOGA

CLARKSVILLE
TEMP FORCE—CLARKSVILLE

CLEVELAND
PREFERRED TEMPORARY SERVICES

CORDOVA
CDI TEMPORARY SERVICES INC

HENDERSONVILLE
EXCLUSIVELY TEMP SERVICE

JACKSON
TEMP FORCE OF JACKSON-
  TENNESSEE

JOHNSON CITY
TEMP FORCE
TEMP FORCE—JOHNSON CITY TN
UNIFORCE TEMPORARY SERVICES

KINGSPORT
SNELLING TEMPORARIES

KNOXVILLE
DUNHILL TEMPORARY SYSTEMS
PERSONNEL POOL OF AMERICA
TEMP SYSTEMS INC

LA VERGNE
HUMAN RESOURCES INC

MARYVILLE
PREFERRED TEMPORARY SERVICES

MEMPHIS
ABLEST SERVICES CORPORATION
ADIA PERSONNEL SERVICES
LEASED LABOR INC
NORRELL SERVICES
PEOPLEMARK INC
PERSONNEL POOL OF AMERICA
SNELLING TEMPORARIES
STAFF BUILDERS

MURFREESBORO
HUMAN RESOURCES INC

NASHVILLE
ABLEST SERVICES CORPORATION
ADIA PERSONNEL SERVICES
AMTEMPS INC
JANE JONES ENTERPRISES INC
NORRELL SERVICES
PERSONNEL POOL OF AMERICA
RESOURCE GROUP INC, THE
TEMPORARY ALTERNATIVES
TODAYS TEMPORARIES
UNIFORCE OF NASHVILLE

SMYRNA
JANE JONES ENTERPRISES

TULLAHOMA
HUMAN RESOURCES INC
NEW HORIZONS SERVICES INC

TEXAS

ABILENE
EXPRESS SERVICES INC

ADDISON
PERSONNEL POOL OF AMERICA

ARLINGTON
ADIA PERSONNEL SERVICES
CDI TEMPORARY SERVICES INC
NORRELL SERVICES
PERSONNEL POOL OF AMERICA
TEAM SERVICES INC
TRC TEMPORARY SERVICES INC

AUSTIN
ADIA PERSONNEL SERVICES
BURNETT PERSONNEL SERVICES
DUNHILL TEMPORARY SYSTEMS
OFFICE SPECIALISTS
PERSONNEL POOL OF AMERICA
TALENT TREE TEMPORARIES
TEMPORARIES INC
TODAYS TEMPORARIES
TRC TEMPORARY SERVICES INC
VOLT TEMPORARY SERVICES

BARKER
PEAKLOAD SERVICES

BEAUMONT
NORRELL SERVICES

BRENHAM
NORRELL SERVICES

CARROLLTON
SNELLING TEMPORARIES

CORPUS CHRISTI
EXPRESS SERVICES INC
MADDEN TEMPORARY SERVICES INC
SNELLING TEMPORARIES

DALLAS
ACCOUNT ABILITIES
ADIA PERSONNEL SERVICES
CDI TEMPORARY SERVICES INC
DURHAM TEMPORARIES INC
FIRSTWORD TEMPORARIES
GROVE TEMPORARIES INC
HIGH PROFILE INC
NORRELL SERVICES
ODESCO TEMPORARIES
OXFORD & ASSOCIATES INC
PEAKLOAD SERVICES
PERSONNEL POOL OF AMERICA
TEAM SERVICES INC
TEMP FORCE OF DALLAS
TEMPO TEMPORARY SERVICE
TEMPORARIES INC

TEMPORARIES NETWORK
TEMPS & CO
TODAYS TEMPORARIES
TRC TEMPORARY SERVICES INC
VOLT TEMPORARY SERVICES
WORDTEMPS INC

DENTON
EXPRESS SERVICES INC

EL PASO
GAIL DARLING TEMPORARIES
NORRELL SERVICES
TEMP FORCE OF EL PASO
TEMPORARIES INC
TRC TEMPORARY SERVICES INC

FORT WORTH
ADIA PERSONNEL SERVICES
NORRELL SERVICES
PEAKLOAD SERVICES
PERSONNEL POOL OF AMERICA
TODAYS TEMPORARY
UNIFORCE TEMPORARY SERVICES
VOLT TEMPORARY SERVICES

GARLAND
GROVE TEMPORARIES INC

HOUSTON
ADIA PERSONNEL SERVICES
AMERICAN SERVICES
BURNETT PERSONNEL SERVICES
CDI TEMPORARY SERVICES INC
HOSPITAL TEMPORARIES
NORRELL SERVICES
OMEGA TEMPORARIES
OXFORD & ASSOCIATES INC
PEAKLOAD SERVICES
PERSONNEL POOL OF AMERICA
QUALITY TEMPORARY SERVICE INC
SKILLMASTER TEMPORARY SERVICES
    INC
SYSTEMP OF TEXAS
TALENT TREE TEMPORARIES
TEMPORARIES INC
TEMPORARIES NETWORK
TEMPS & CO
TRACY TEMPORARIES INC

HOUSTON HEIGHTS
PERSONNEL POOL OF AMERICA

HURST
TEMPS & CO

IRVING
ADIA PERSONNEL SERVICES
CDI TEMPORARY SERVICES INC
NORRELL SERVICES
PERSONNEL POOL OF AMERICA
SELECT TEMPORARIES INC
TEAM SERVICES INC
TEMPS & CO

TODAYS TEMPORARIES
TRC TEMPORARY SERVICES INC
VOLT TEMPORARY SERVICES

JACKSONVILLE
NORRELL SERVICES

LUBBOCK
SNELLING TEMPORARIES

MIDLAND
ADIA PERSONNEL SERVICES
TEMP TIME

ODESSA
ADIA PERSONNEL SERVICES

PASADENA
BRUCO TEMPORARY SERVICES

PLANO
CDI TEMPORARY SERVICES INC

RICHARDSON
ADIA PERSONNEL SERVICES
TODAYS TEMPORARIES
TRC TEMPORARY SERVICES INC

SAN ANTONIO
ADIA PERSONNEL SERVICES
CDI TEMPORARY SERVICES INC
DUNHILL TEMPORARY SYSTEMS
DURHAM TEMPORARIES INC
EXPRESS SERVICES INC
NORRELL SERVICES
PEAKLOAD SERVICES
PERSONNEL POOL OF AMERICA
SELECT TEMPORARIES INC
TEMPORARIES INC
TODAYS TEMPORARIES

TEMPLE
EXPRESS SERVICES INC
NORRELL SERVICES
PERSONNEL POOL OF AMERICA

TYLER
MANPOWER INC

WACO
EXPRESS SERVICES INC
NORRELL SERVICES

WICHITA FALLS
EXPRESS SERVICES INC

UTAH

MURRAY
SOS TEMPORARY SERVICES

OGDEN
SOS TEMPORARY SERVICES

OREM
SOS TEMPORARY SERVICES

SALT LAKE CITY
ARROW AND AND-EX TEMPORARY
 HELP
EXPRESS SERVICES INC
SOS TEMPORARY SERVICES
TEMP FORCE OF SALT LAKE CITY
VOLT TEMPORARY SERVICES

SANDY
ADIA PERSONNEL SERVICES

VERMONT

ARLINGTON
HERITAGE TEMPORARIES

BRATTLEBORO
HARMON TEMPORARY SERVICE

BURLINGTON
THE 500 RECRUITERS

WILLISTON
TRIAD TEMPORARY SERVICES INC

VIRGINIA

ALEXANDRIA
ADIA PERSONNEL SERVICES
EDITORIAL EXPERTS INC
NATIONAL ASSOCIATION OF
 TEMPORARY SERVICES INC
NORRELL SERVICES
TEMP FORCE OF ALEXANDRIA
TRACY TEMPORARIES INC

ANNANDALE
FORBES TEMPORARIES INC
NORRELL SERVICES

ARLINGTON
BSI TEMPORARIES INC
DUNHILL TEMPORARY SYSTEMS
NAIOP
PERSONNEL POOL OF AMERICA
TEMPORARIES INC

AYLETT
ALL AMERICAN PROFESSIONAL
 SERVICES INC

BAILEYS CROSSROADS
TEMPORARY RESOURCES

BLACKSBURG
NORRELL SERVICES

CHARLOTTESVILLE
SNELLING TEMPORARIES

FAIRFAX
GOODFRIEND TEMPORARY SERVICES
OXFORD & ASSOCIATES INC

FALLS CHURCH
ADIA PERSONNEL SERVICES
ADVANTAGE INC
GOODFRIEND TEMPORARY SERVICES
NORRELL SERVICES
TELE SEC TEMPORARY SERVICES
UNIFORCE TEMPORARY SERVICES

GLEN ALLEN
SELECT TEMPORARY SERVICES

HAMPTON
CDI TEMPORARY SERVICES INC
PROTEMPS TEMPORARY SERVICES
SELECT TEMPORARY SERVICES

LYNCHBURG
AMERISTAFF COMPANIES INC
NORRELL SERVICES

MANASSAS
TEMPORARY SOLUTIONS

MARTINSVILLE
AMERISTAFF COMPANIES INC

MCLEAN
ADVANTAGE TEMPORARY SERVICES
GOODFRIEND TEMPORARY SERVICES
INTERSEC PERSONNEL SERVICE
MONARCH TEMPORARY SVCS (TS)
SELECT TEMPORARY SERVICES
SPARKS PERSONNEL SERVICES INC
TEMPORARIES INC

NEWPORT NEWS
ADIA PERSONNEL SERVICES
LEE TEMPS ASSOCIATES INC
NORRELL SERVICES

NORFOLK
CDI TEMPORARY SERVICES INC
GRESS ASSOCIATES INC
NORRELL SERVICES
PROTEMPS TEMPORARY SERVICES
SELECT TEMPORARY SERVICES
SNELLING TEMPORARIES
TODAYS TEMPORARIES

RESTON
CDI TEMPORARY SERVICES INC
FORBES TEMPORARIES INC
GOODFRIEND TEMPORARY SERVICES

MONARCH TEMPORARY SVCS (TS)
NORRELL SERVICES
SELECT TEMPORARY SERVICES
SPARKS PERSONNEL SERVICES INC
TELESEC TEMPORARY SERVICES
TEMPORARY EXCHANGE

RICHMOND
ABACUS TEMPORARY SERVICES
ADIA PERSONNEL SERVICES
ALL AMERICAN PROFESSIONAL
 SERVICES INC
BATTELLE TEMPS INC
CDI TEMPORARY SERVICES INC
CTS INC
NORRELL SERVICES
PERSONNEL POOL OF AMERICA
SELECT TEMPORARY SERVICES
SNELLING TEMPORARIES
STAFF BUILDERS
TEMPORARY RESOURCES
TRACY TEMPORARIES INC

ROANOKE
ADIA PERSONNEL SERVICES
NORRELL SERVICES

SOUTH BOSTON
PAPER TIGERS INC

SPRINGFIELD
GOODFRIEND TEMPORARY SERVICES

STAUNTON
JOBSHOP INC

VIENNA
ADIA PERSONNEL SERVICES
AMERITEMPS
BSI TEMPORARIES INC
DUNHILL TEMPORARY SYSTEMS
PRN NURSING TEMPS INC
TEMPORARY PLACEMENT INCORP
TEMPORARY RESOURCES
VOLT TEMPORARY SERVICES
WOODSIDE EMPLOYMENT
 CONSULTANTS INC

VIRGINIA BEACH
ABACUS SERVICES INC
ADIA PERSONNEL SERVICES
ALL AMERICAN PROFESSIONAL
 SERVICES INC
PROTEMPS TEMPORARY SERVICES
SELECT TEMPORARY SERVICES
UNIFORCE TEMPORARY SERVICES

WILLIAMSBURG
PROTEMPS TEMPORARY SERVICES

WINCHESTER
ACTION EXECUTIVE SERVICES INC
ADIA PERSONNEL SERVICES

WASHINGTON

BELLEVUE
VOLT TEMPORARY SERVICES

BREMERTON
EXPRESS SERVICES INC

CENTRALIA
TWIN CITY PERSONNEL SERVICE

CHEHALIS
EXPRESS SERVICES INC

EVERETT
EXPRESS SERVICES INC

FEDERAL WAY
PERSONNEL POOL OF AMERICA
VOLT TEMPORARY SERVICES

KENNEWICK
EXPRESS SERVICES INC

KENT
EXPRESS SERVICES INC

LACEY
EMPLOYMENT NORTHWEST INC

LYNNWOOD
EXPRESS SERVICES INC
VOLT TEMPORARY SERVICES

MOSES LAKE
TEMPORARY ALTERNATIVES INC

OLYMPIA
EXPRESS SERVICES INC

REDMOND
EXPRESS SERVICES INC
PERSONNEL POOL OF AMERICA

RENTON
VOLT TEMPORARY SERVICES

SEATTLE
ACCOUNTING FORCE INC
ADIA PERSONNEL SERVICES
DUNHILL TEMPORARY SYSTEMS
PERSONNEL POOL OF AMERICA
PREFERRED
   TEMPORARIES/TECHSTAF
SNELLING TEMPORARIES
STAFF BUILDERS
TEMPORARIES INC
UNITED TEMPORARY SERVICES INC
VOLT TEMPORARY SERVICES

SPOKANE
EXPRESS SERVICES INC

TACOMA
ADIA PERSONNEL SERVICES
EVERGREEN TEMPORARIES
EXPRESS SERVICES INC
PERSONNEL POOL OF AMERICA

VANCOUVER
K-M TEMPORARY SERVICES
PERSONNEL POOL OF AMERICA

WENATCHEE
ADD TEMPORARY HELP SERVICE
EXPRESS SERVICES INC

YAKIMA
ADD TEMPORARY HELP SERVICE
EXPRESS SERVICES INC

WEST VIRGINIA

CHARLESTON
SMART TEMPORARY SERVICES

PARKERSBURG
NORRELL SERVICES
X-TRAS

WISCONSIN

APPLETON
FLEX-STAFF TEMPORARY SERVICES
NORRELL SERVICES

BELOIT
DEPENDABILITY

BROOKFIELD
ADIA PERSONNEL SERVICES
OMEGA TEMPORARIES

BROWN DEER
NORRELL SERVICES

FORT ATKINSON
TERRA TEMPORARY PERSONNEL

GREEN BAY
NORRELL SERVICES

HARTFORD
BOYD-HUNTER INC

KENOSHA
MERRICK TEMPORARY SERVICES

MADISON
AMERICAN BUSINESS RESOURCE
   CORPORATION
NORRELL SERVICES

MANITOWOC
AMERICAN BUSINESS RESOURCE
   CORPORATION

MILWAUKEE
ADIA PERSONNEL SERVICES
CROWN SERVICES
DUNHILL TEMPORARY SYSTEMS
FLEXI-FORCE TEMP SVCS
MANPOWER TEMPORARY SERVICES
PERSONNEL POOL OF AMERICA
TAD TEMPORARIES
TEMP FORCE—MILWAUKEE WI
TEMPSPLUS TEMPORARY SVCS INC

SHEBOYGAN
AMERICAN BUSINESS RESOURCE
   CORPORATION

STEVENS POINT
AMERICAN BUSINESS RESOURCE
   CORPORATION

STURGEON BAY
AMERICAN BUSINESS RESOURCE
   CORPORATION

WAUWATOSA
ADIA PERSONNEL SERVICES
DUNHILL TEMPORARY SYSTEMS
NORRELL SERVICES

WYOMING

CASPER
ARROW AND AND-EX TEMPORARY
   HELP
EXPRESS SERVICES INC

CHEYENNE
EXPRESS SERVICES INC

DIRECTORY OF EMPLOYMENT AGENCIES WITH TEMPORARY SERVICES, BY STATE AND CITY

The following directory is a listing of permanent employment agencies that also offer a temporary help division. This may be particularly helpful to job seekers who are seeking temporary employment in order to secure a permanent position. The services listed here are part of The Temporary Help Section of The National Association of Personnel Consultants (NAPC). NAPC is headquartered at Roundhouse Square, 1423 Duke Street, Alexandria, Virginia 22314, phone number 703-684-0180. NAPC has national membership of over 2,000 firms, a portion of which are in the temporary help business. We reprint this list with its permission.

ALABAMA

Career Personnel Service
Montgomery, AL

Employment Consultants, Inc.
Montgomery, AL

ALASKA

Offices Unlimited, Inc.
Anchorage, AK

CALIFORNIA

ITT Employer Services
Encino, CA

PIPS Personnel Services
Long Beach, CA

Harding Personnel Services
Ontario, CA

TPS Agency
Redding, CA

Redlands Employment Agency
Redlands, CA

Prestige Personnel
Rowland Heights, CA

Eastridge Personnel Services
San Diego, CA

Abar Personnel
San Francisco, CA

Alper and Associates
San Francisco, CA

Key Personnel Services
San Francisco, CA

Mark Associates
San Francisco, CA

Citywide Personnel Service
Santa Barbara, CA

Select Temporaries, Inc.
Santa Barbara, CA

Justin-Bentley Agency
Torrance, CA

Capricorn Personnel Service
West Hollywood, CA

Dial Personnel Associates
Whittier, CA

COLORADO

Express Personnel Service
Boulder, CO

CONNECTICUT

Charter Personnel Services
Danbury, CT

Northeast Personnel Resources
Danbury, CT

Gambrill & Associates, Inc.
Darien, CT

Dunhill Temporary Systems,
   Inc.
East Hartford, CT

Personnel Priorities
Essex, CT

Gilbert Lane Personnel
Hamden, CT

Gilbert Lane Personnel Agency
Hartford, CT

RJS Associates, Inc.
Hartford, CT

A. R. Mazzotta Associates
Middletown, CT

Diversified Employment Service
New Haven, CT

Hipp Waters Office Personnel
Stamford, CT

Judlind Associates
Stamford, CT

Lewis Personnel Inc.
Stamford, CT

Jaci Carroll Personnel Service
Waterbury, CT

Uni/Search of Waterbury, Inc.
Waterbury, CT

The Hire Group
West Hartford, CT

DISTRICT OF COLUMBIA

Alden Atwood and Associates
Washington, DC

CompeTemps By Dora, Inc.
Washington, DC

Medical Personnel Service
Washington, DC

FLORIDA

Richard Rita Personnel
Lakeland, FL

Star Personnel
Miami, FL

Landrum Personnel Associates
Pensacola, FL

Snelling and Snelling, Inc.
Sarasota, FL

David Wood Personnel
West Palm Beach, FL

GEORGIA

Lawstaf, Inc.
Atlanta, GA

Sara Burden/Office Staffing
Atlanta, GA

Talent Force Temporaries
Atlanta, GA

HAWAII

Associated Employment Services
Honolulu, HI

IDAHO

Pro Staff Services
Boise, ID

ILLINOIS

Banner Personnel Service
Chicago, IL

Executemps, Inc.
Chicago, IL

Profile Temporary Service, Inc.
Chicago, IL

Thirty Three Personnel Center
Chicago, IL

Prestige Personnel
Homewood, IL

The Murphy Group
Oak Brook, IL

Matthews Professional
Waukegan, IL

C. Berger & Company
Wheaton, IL

INDIANA

Alpha Rae Personnel, Inc.
Fort Wayne, IN

IOWA

Job Finders, Inc.
Des Moines, IA

LOUISIANA

Dunhill Personnel of Jefferson
Metairie, LA

Holly Employment Service
Monroe, LA

MASSACHUSETTS

Andover Personnel
Andover, MA

Active Personnel Consultants
Boston, MA

Daniel Roberts Associates
Boston, MA

Travel People Personnel
Boston, MA

WPC
Boston, MA

Technical Job-Solver, Inc.
Chelsea, MA

Pro Search Personnel
S. Dennis, MA

Gilbert Lane Personnel Service
Springfield, MA

United Temporaries
Springfield, MA

Barclay Personnel Systems
Woburn, MA

Scott James Associates, Inc.
Worcester, MA

Mass Paramedical Registry
Worcester, MA

MARYLAND

Silver Employment Service
Baltimore, MD

Bookkeeper Plus, Inc.
Gaithersburg, MD

Karen Smith Temps, Inc.
Wheaton, MD

MINNESOTA

Dennhardt & Associates
Bloomington, MN

Temp Center, Inc.
Bloomington, MN

Office Consultants
Golden Valley, MN

Andcor Companies, Inc.
Minneapolis, MN

MISSISSIPPI

Blackley & Blackley Personnel
Greenville, MS

Tatum Personnel
Jackson, MS

MISSOURI

Professional Career
Development
Kansas City, MO

Professional Career
Development
St. Louis, MO

First Place, Inc.
Springfield, MO

MONTANA

Career Quest
Great Falls, MT

NEBRASKA

Personnel Search
Omaha, NE

NEVADA

Westwind Associates
Las Vegas, NV

All Nevada Employment
Sparks, NV

NEW HAMPSHIRE

Woodbury Personnel Consultants
Concord, NH

Exeter 2100
Hampton, NH

Chesire Employment Service
Keene, NH

NEW JERSEY

The Linton Companies
Berlin, NJ

Applied Personnel
East Brunswick, NJ

Dunhill Personnel of Middlesex
Edison, NJ

Citizens Employment Service
Fort Lee, NJ

Arline Simpson Associates
Hackensack, NJ

Munson Placement Services,
   Inc.
Lawrenceville, NJ

Normann Personnel Consultants
Paramus, NJ

Blair Personnel Service
Parsippany, NJ

The Hartshorn Group
Parsippany, NJ

Town Systems
Piscataway, NJ

Gerotoga-A-1 In Personnel
Scotch Plains, NJ

NEW MEXICO

Roadrunner Employment
   Services
Albuquerque, NM

NEW YORK

Wylie Associates, Inc.
Buffalo, NY

CPA Associates Personnel, Inc.
Dewitt, NY

Lloyd Personnel Consultants
Great Neck, NY

Globalforce Personnel, Inc.
Melville, NY

Accountancy Personnel, Inc.
New York, NY

Continental Word Processing
New York, NY

Lawrence Temporary Services
New York, NY

Sloan Personnel
New York, NY

Walker Associates
New York, NY

Winmar Personnel Agency
New York, NY

Career Placements/Tempforce
Westbury, NY

Corporate Temps
White Plains, NY

Carrie Allen & Associates
Williamsville, NY

NORTH CAROLINA

Action Personnel Services
Charlotte, NC

Creative Personnel Services
Charlotte, NC

Nationwide Personnel
Fayetteville, NC

Personnel Temp of Forest City
Forest City, NC

Action Personnel/Gastonia Inc.
Gastonia, NC

Graham & Associates
   Employment Consultants
Greensboro, NC

Jan-Ker Inc.
Greensboro, NC

The Personnel Center
Greensboro, NC

Regency Personnel Consultants
Greensboro, NC

Anne's Temporaries, Inc.
Greenville, NC

The Personnel Center
Highpoint, NC

TPS of Monroe, Inc.
Monroe, NC

OHIO

Timblin Personnel
Akron, OH

Egar Employment
Beachwood, OH

Le-Gals Career Corner
Cleveland, OH

Flowers and Associates
Maumee, OH

Interconnect Technical Service
Toledo, OH

OKLAHOMA

Dunhill Personnel Tulsa
Tulsa, OK

Lloyd Richards Personnel
Service
Tulsa, OK

OREGON

AAAA Temporary Services, Inc.
Portland, OR

Alpine Consultants
Portland, OR

Murphy, Symonds and Stowell
Portland, OR

PENNSYLVANIA

EDCO Personnel Systems, Inc.
Audubon, PA

J-Rand Personnel, Inc.
Bethlehem, PA

Triangle Associates
Fort Washington, PA

Keystone Personnel
Lemoyne, PA

Eagle Staffers and Placers Inc.
Media, PA

McCallion Associates, Inc.
Montgomeryville, PA

Ames Personnel Services
Philadelphia, PA

Accounting Personnel Associates
Pittsburgh, PA

American Business Center
Pittsburgh, PA

Liken Services
Pittsburgh, PA

Gordon Wahls Company
Villanova, PA

Snelling and Snelling
Williamsport, PA

The BYRNES Group
York, PA

Employment East, Inc.
York, PA

SOUTH CAROLINA

Business Force, Inc.
Columbia, SC

Godshall & Godshall Personnel
Consultants
Greenville, SC

Smith Personnel, Inc.
Hilton Head Island, SC

Special Personnel
Hilton Head Island, SC

Personnel Inc.
Spartanburg, SC

TENNESSEE

Heritage Personnel Service
Johnson City, TN

Accountants and Bookkeepers
Memphis, TN

TEXAS

Burnett's Southwest Personnel
Arlington, TX

Robert Half of Dallas
Dallas, TX

Addington Personnel
Houston, TX

Talent Tree Personnel Service
Houston, TX

J. Robert Thompson Companies
Houston, TX

Bruco Personnel Services, Inc.
Pasadena, TX

Adia Personnel Services
San Antonio, TX

Prestige Personnel Consultants
Texarkana, TX

VIRGINIA

Carol Maden Personnel
Hampton, VA

Lee Recruiters
Newport News, VA

JobShop, Inc.
Staunton, VA

WASHINGTON

Pace Network, Inc.
Bellevue, WA

INDEX

AARP (American Association of Retired Persons), 9
accountants, 11, 34, 37
Accountemps, 37
accumulated hours, and benefits, 60
actors, 8–9
adaptability anxiety, 86
Adia Personnel Services, 3
Administrative Management Society, 12, 92
advertisements
   for part-time employment, 91
   recruitment, 40
advertising agencies, 22
Age Discrimination in Employment Act of 1967, 65
aging, of labor force, 12
AIDS, 30
aliens, illegal, 46
American Association of Retired Persons (AARP), 9
anxiety, adaptability, 86
application, 45, 46, 61

artists, 1, 8–9
assignment managers, 47
   tips from, 50–51
   relationship with, 52
assignments
   best and worst of, 80–81
   accepting, 51
   cancelling, 51
   hatred of, 55, 57
   length of, 51
   pressure to take, 52
attendance bonus, 64
attitude, 50, 71
   of coworkers, 53–54
   "just-a-temp", 82–83
   about typing, 44
attorneys, 1, 11, 35–37, 75–76
automated office, 8, 12, 20

Balsamo, Anthony, on technical temps, 31
banking, 22
Beaulieu, Lorraine, 79

benefits, *see* fringe benefits
Boardroom Reports, 16
bonding, of temporary workers, 15
bonuses, 64
boredom, 86
Bosco, Casey, 76
budgeting, 74
  for temporary help, 11
burn out, 7, 27
business school, 25

Cameron, Ronald, on pharmacists as
  temps, 38
Cameron & Company, 38
Candid Camera, 80
Career Blazers, 25, 50
Career Blazers Handbook, 59
career choice, 1
career-conscious, 40
career path, 87
career temps, 10, 72–73
Cartwright, Elaine, on temporary work
  advantages, 7
certified public accountants, 2, 78
checklists, reasons-to-temp, 13–14
chemists, 11
child-care providers, 38
child-care reimbursement, 64
children, 7, 45
Christmas parties, 17
civil rights laws, 65
Clarke, Tina, 79
classified ads, 42, 91
  as source of salary information, 23
clerical help, 19
  see also office personnel
clients, 53–55
  fee payment by, 14
  information about, 50
  permanent job offer from, 58
  for self-employed, 96
  service follow-up calls to, 54
code of ethics, 66
Collard, Judie, 74–75, 83
college graduates, 1, 7–8
Commission for Human Rights, state, 66

communication skills, 72
companions, as home health-care occupations, 30
competence, technical, 76
competition, for jobs, 7
Comprehensive Health Systems, Inc., 35
computer software, 76
  requests for, 21
  training on, 24
computer specialists, 11, 39
computerization, 20
  see also automated office
Conference Board, 90
consultants, 40, 71, 72
contract help, 34
contracting, temporary, 39
contracting leasing firm, 94
contractors, independent, 94–96
conversion teams, for computerization,
  20
corporate internship, temporary work as,
  7
Cosmopolitan Care Corporation, 29
costs, of employee recruitment, 14
coworkers, 84
  attitudes of, 53–54
  and pay rates, 57
  see also permanent employees
credit union, 65
cross-training, 90
Culver, Bruce, on scientists as temps, 38
custodial patient care, 30
customer service personnel, 1

damages, liquidated, 58
data-base management system, 22
data-base skills, 21
data entry skills, 21
dBase III, 21
Debbie Temps, 25, 65
defense work, 30
Deficit Reduction Act of 1984, 94
DeLeyer, Anna Marie, 1, 72–73
Denecour, Ron, 73–74
designers, 30
desktop publishing, 22

diagnosis related groups (DRGs), 29
Dictionary of Temporary Help, 3
Dillon, April, 77
direct mail, 40
disability, 5
discrimination, 65
disposable employment force, 17
doctors, 11
  as temporary workers, 34
documentation, of employment eligibil-
    ity, 46
drafters, 30
dress for interview with service, 45
DRGs (diagnosis related groups), 29

economy
  industry- vs. service-based, 33
  recession in, 11
EDP/MIS contractors, 31
EEO (Equal Employment Opportunity)
    Commission, 66
Ekwurzel, Nita, 38
electronic spreadsheet, 21, 22
electronic typewriters, 22–23
emergency replacement calls, 85
emergency staffing needs, 6
employee leasing, 93–94
employee recruitment costs, 14
employee representative, 47
employer, of temporary workers, 5–6
employment, part-time, 90–91
  see also permanent employment; tem-
    porary employment
employment agencies, 42
  temporary help service affiliation with,
    16
employment agreement, 62
employment eligibility, documentation
    of, 46
Employment Verification System, 46
encoder operator, 103
Encore! program of Kelly Services, 9
engineering, 34
engineers, 11, 30
entry-level positions, 7, 22

Equal Employment Opportunity (EEO)
    Commission, 66
Equal Pay Act of 1963, 65
error probability, of industrial employees,
    28
errors and omissions insurance, 15
estimated taxes, 95
ethics code, 66
executive assistants, 2
experience, and pay rate, 23–24
eye contact, in interview, 47

Fair Employment Practices Agency of
    states, 66
Fair Labor Standards Act, 66
Fallon, Leslie, 2, 70–71
favors, asking for and receiving, 51–53
fee, collection of, 73
feedback, 54
FICA (Social Security), 5, 9
  for self-employed, 95
financial insecurity, 74
flexibility, 13, 15, 16, 74, 76
  in staffing, 6
flexible work schedules, 92
flexitime, 92
floaters, 89–90
Florida International University, 24
foreign languages, 25
forms, sample, 59–60
free-lancers, 40, 95
fringe benefits, 5, 14, 17, 31, 60–65, 74
  lack of, 83–84

Geyer-McAllister Publications, Inc., 22
gift program, 64
government contracts, 31
Grady, Susan, on disadvantages of tempo-
    rary work, 17

handouts, 59–60, 62
health care personnel, temporary, 6
  see also doctors; nurses
health insurance, 17, 31, 60, 84
health-care aides, 30
health-care companies, 22

health-care legislation, 65
hidden job market, 9
holiday pay, 64
home health care, 28–30
hospitals, 28
hours, accumulation of, and benefits, 60
Hueneke, Terry
  on office skill demand, 21
  on temporary worker qualifications, 15

I-9 form (Immigration and Naturalization
    Service), 46
IBM DisplayWrite, 21
ill employees, temporary help to replace,
    12
illegal aliens, 46
illegal requests from client, 55–57
illustrators, 1
Immigration and Naturalization Service,
    I-9 form, 46
Immigration Reform and Control Act of
    1986, 46
income
  guarantees of, 35
  supplementing, 16
  see also pay rate
independent contractors, 94–96
independents, 40
industrial/labor temps, 6, 27–28
industry-based economy, 33
information, obtaining, 53
insurance, 5, 14, 22
  for bonding temps, 15
  errors and omissions, 15
  health, 17, 31, 60, 64, 84
  unemployment, 14
internal pools, 89–90
internship, corporate, temporary work
    as, 7
interviews, 40, 42, 45, 47–48
inventory clerk, 103
inventory of skills, 42
isolation, 17, 84–85

Jarett, Andrew R., on lawyers as temps,
    36

job descriptions, 3
  see also occupational titles
job-hopping, 12
job hunters, 2, 9–10
job market, hidden, 9
job openings, unadvertised, 9–10
jobs, competition for, 7
job search, 16
job sharing, 92–93
job shops, 30

Kelly Services, Inc., 9
  training by, 24–25
Kennedy, James, 71–72
Kenyon, Helene, 65
  on training, 25
Klarreich, Joel, on nurses, 29
KRON Medical Corporation, 34
Kronhaus, Alan, on doctors as temps, 34

labor force
  disposable, 17
  reentry into, 8
  and temporary worker growth, 12
labor intermediary, temporary help ser-
    vice as, 6
labor shortage, 6
Lab Support, 38
Landon, Molly, on medical temporary
    employment, 30
law, 22, 34
Lawsmiths, 35, 36
laws, civil rights, 65
Law/temps, 36
lawyers, 1, 11, 35–37, 75–76
layoffs, 11
learning–curve factor, 90
leasing, employee, 93–94
length of assignments, 51
letters, from clients, 54
liquidated damages, 58
locum tenens, 34
Locum Tenens, Inc., 34, 35
longevity bonus, 64
Lotus 1-2-3, 21

mailing lists, 40
malpractice, 35
management styles, 11
Manpower, Inc., 15, 21
  training program of, 25
manufacturers, 27
marketing temps, 26–27
markup, by temporary help service, 14
Marolda, Tony, 39
McLoughlin, Jerry, 2, 78
medical insurance, 17, 31, 60, 64, 84
medical temps, 28–30
Medicare/Medicaid, 28–29
medicine, 34
mentor, 16
merit increase, 64
metropolitan area, temporary help ser-
    vice in, 44
Microsoft Word, 21
Minimum Essential Health-Care Act, 65
minimum wage, 66
mobility, of labor force, 12
Moore, Herb, 1
mothers, working, 6–7
Multimate, 21
Multiplan, 21
musicians, 8–9

National Association of Personnel Consul-
    tants, 3
National Association of Temporary Ser-
    vices (NATS), 3, 66
national organizations, 44
negotiation, of higher pay rate, 58–59
nest egg, 2
network, 96
Newmark, Stan, 37
newspapers
  part-time employment ads in, 91
  recruitment ads in, 40
New York Times, 21
night work, 77
no-show temps, 51
notepad, 53
nurses, 1
  temporary, 29

nurse's aides, 1
nursing homes, 28

Occupational Outlook Quarterly, 32
occupational titles
  for medical temporary workers, 30
  for office workers, 19–20
  for technology temporary workers, 31
  for temporary industrial workers, 28
Office, 22
Office Administration and Automation,
    22
office automation skills, 45
office personnel
  forecasted growth and demand for, 20
  salary survey for, 23
  temporary, 6, 19–26
office politics, 71
Office Publications, Inc., 22
office skills, demand for, 21–23
office visits, to temporary help service,
    44
older workers, 73–74
one-time projects, 12
open houses, by temporary help services,
    40
Ostrander, Joyce, on training, 24
overtime pay, 14, 66
overtime work, 28

PageMaker, 21
parents, working, 6–7
part-time employment, 90–91
pay, overtime, 14, 66
pay check
  picking up, 51–52
  stubs of, 62
payday, 42
payment, for temporary lawyers, 37
pay rate, 50
  city vs. suburbs, 44
  discussing with permanent employees,
    57–58
  negotiating higher, 58–59
  survey of, 23
payrolling, 9, 94

pay scale, 71
PC Magazine, 22
PC station, 20
PCW Communications, Inc., 22
PC World, 22
pensions, 94
  supplementing, 9
performance reports, 54
permanent employees, 67–68
  getting dumped on by, 85–86
  and pay rate discussion, 57–58
  see also coworkers
permanent employment, 40, 42
  and benefits, 60
  offer of, from client, 58
  temporary work and, 7, 9–10, 16, 87
personal computer operators, 2
personal computers, definition of, 22
personal time, 71
Peyton, Bruce, on lack of benefits, 83
pharmacists, 2, 38, 70–71
Physicians Relief Network, 35
pirating, 58
Pitts, Jerry, 80
pools, internal, 89–90
power, limitations on, 86–87
practical joker, 69
Press, Susan, 73
privately-owned temporary help services,
  45
private-sector business, temporary help
  service as, 6
probability for error, of industrial employees, 28
problem solver, 86
productivity, 28
professional temps, 1, 10–11, 33–40
profit sharing, 2, 78
proximity, 16

quality control, 46

Ragan, Patti, on training, 24
raise, 59
real estate firms, 22
recession, economic, 11
recommendations, 42

recruitment
  ads for, 40
  costs of, 14
  of temporary workers, 14
reentry into labor force, 8
references, 14, 45, 77
referral bonus, 64
Rego, Albert, 76
Rent-A-Consultant, 39
repetitive tasks, and probability of error,
  28
replacement calls, emergency, 85
respect, from peers, 76
responsibility, 86
  upgrading of, 23
resume, 45, 46
  temporary employment listed on, 88
retired persons, 2, 9, 78
rules, handout on, 62

salary survey, office, 23, 24
sample forms, 59–60
Santa Claus, 27
Schlender-Way, Debbie, 74
science, 34
scientists, 37–38
screening, of temporary workers, 14
seasonal needs, temporary help for, 12
securities, 22
self-employed, 95
self-image, 83
self-paced training, 25
senior-level executives, 11
service-based economy, 33
severance, 14
severance costs, 11
sex discrimination, 65
shortage of labor, 6
skills
  building, 8
  demand for, 44
  inventory of, 42
Skillware, 25
small business, 93
Smith, John, on doctors as temps, 34
social isolation, 17, 84–85

Social Security (FICA), 5, 9
    for self-employed, 95
software packages, 76
    requests for, 21
    training on, 24
special assignments, 51
spreadsheets, 21, 22
staffing, emergency need for, 6
standby temporary workers, 85
Star Temps, 24
state agencies, 66
statistics, on temporary employment, 2
status, 40, 76
    of temporary workers, 1
stereotypical temporary workers, 11
stress, 72, 74, 76, 86
strike breaking, 17–18
students, 7–8
suburbs, temporary help service in, 44
Symphony, 21

Tax Equity and Fiscal Responsibility Act
    (TEFRA) of 1982, 94
taxes, withholding, for self-employed, 95
Technical Aid Corporation, 31
technical competence, 76
technical temps, 30–32
technical/professional temporary workers,
    6
technology, 12
telephone answering machine, 50, 51, 96
telephone calls, to temporary help ser-
    vice, 42, 48, 70, 85
telephone directory, 39–40, 42
Temp Careers, Inc., 24
temp counselor, 47, 73, 77–78
temp dispatcher, 47
temp industry
    functioning of, 14–15
    growth of, 12
temping, definition of, 5–6
temp mama, 68
temp manager, 47
temporary contracting, 39
temporary employment, 1
    advantages of, for individual, 13–14

    alternatives to, 89–96
    categories of, 19
    classes of, 5
    as credible work experience, 87
    disadvantages of, 17–18
    factors affecting growth of, 2
    listing of, on resume, 88
    positive aspects of, 16–17
    problems of, 82–88
    pros and cons of, 40
    statistics on, 2
temporary help service, 5
    affiliation with employment agency, 16
    characteristics of, 6
    choosing, 41–48
    locating, 39–40
    markup by, 14
    national vs. local privately-owned, 45
    number of, 11
    obligations to, 73
    office visits to, 44, 45
    problems of, 10
    questions to ask, 47
    registering with, 48
    relationship with, 41–66
    telephone calls to, 42, 70
temporary workers
    average expenditures for, 15
    bonding of, 15
    budgeting for, 11
    career, 10
    characteristics of, 6–11
    characteristics of good, 15–16
    frequency of use of, 12
    full-time, 10
    industrial, 27–28
    life as, 67–81
    marketing, 26–27
    medical, 28–30
    no-show, 51
    office, 19–26
    professional, 10–11, 33–40
    profiles of, 69–80
    reasons for using, 12–13
    recruitment of, 14
    rights of, 65–66
    standby, 85

temporary workers (*continued*)
  status of, 1
  stereotypical, 11
  technical, 30–32
  working with, 50
testing, 45–46
text processing, 21
time sheet, 58, 63
trade publications, 21–22
  recruitment ads in, 40
trade show exhibits, 26
training, from temporary help firm, 20, 22, 23–26, 27, 64, 72
Trotter, Deborah, 75–76
turnaround, in temp industry, 14
typewriters, 22–23
typing, 22
  attitude about, 44

unadvertised job openings, 9–10
unemployment insurance, 14
unethical requests from client, 57
U.S. Bureau of Labor Statistics, 2, 27–28
U.S. Department of Health and Human Services, 29
U.S. Department of Labor, 66

vacation, 1, 60, 62, 64
variety, 71

wages
  discrimination in, 65
  minimum, 66
  see also pay rate

Walker, Eric, 35
Webster, Robert, 35
Websterss, Ghenia, 2, 53, 69–70
Weiner, Robert, 36
Western Marketing Services, 26
Western's University of Santa Claus, 27
Western Temporary Services of California, 26
withholding taxes, for self-employed, 95
women, reentry of, into labor force, 8
women's movement, 12
word processing, 8, 20, 21
  on personal computers, 22
WordPerfect, 21
WordStar, 21
work
  availability of, 85
  quantity of, 54
workday, control of, 4
work environment, 10
worker's compensation, 5
work experience, temporary employment as, 87
workforce, *see* labor force
working nomads, 17
working parents, 6–7, 74–75
work schedules, flexible, 92
writers, 8–9

Xerox Corporation, 20

Yellow Pages, 39–40, 42

Ziff-Davis Publishing Co., 22
Zink, Jenny, on marketing temps, 26–27